Yours &c.
J. Clay

ANNALS

OF THE

SWEDES ON THE DELAWARE,

FROM THEIR

FIRST SETTLEMENT IN 1636,

TO

THE PRESENT TIME,

BY THE

REV. JEHU CURTIS CLAY, D. D.

Rector of Gloria Dei Church, Philadelphia.

SECOND EDITION, CORRECTED AND ENLARGED.

PHILADELPHIA:
H. HOOKER & CO., EIGHTH AND CHESTNUT STS.
1858.

M'Farland & Thomson, Printers,
311 Walnut St.

PREFACE.

This book is presented to the public under the following circumstances. The compiler, descended on the mother's side from Swedish ancestors, felt a desire to look back into their history, and to know more than he did of the occurrences connected with their first settlement on this soil. He had observed that the geographers and historians of America, while they had been very particular in detailing the circumstances connected with the arrival and settlement of the English on the James River, and of the Pilgrims in New England, had scarcely mentioned that there was ever such a colony as the Swedes on the Delaware. He was at a loss to know why this was so; especially as their arrival here was about thirty years after that of the English in Virginia, and but about sixteen or seventeen years after the settlement of New England; and that, therefore, their being among the first colonies that came from Europe to America, and the very first that settled Pennsylvania, claimed for them a more particular notice. It is true, Proud in his

History of Pennsylvania, Smith in his History of New Jersey, and Holmes in his American Annals, have spoken of the arrival of the Swedes on the Delaware. And, some may ask, what more do we wish to know of them? As much more—their many descendants now living, if no others, will answer—as may throw light on their early history, show the relation in which they stood to the people around them, the connection they had with, and the protection they received from, the country whence they came; and the various changes, civil and ecclesiastical, through which they had to pass. Of all these matters their own historians have given full and interesting details. To those details the present writer has given much of his attention; and deeply interested as he has been himself in the inquiry, he has been led to think it would be a gratification, to at least the many among us who derive their descent from Swedish ancestors, to have the most prominent points of the history of their forefathers selected from the volumes and manuscripts where they lie embedded with much that is of no value, and offered to their perusal.

The writers to whom we are chiefly indebted for information concerning the first settlement and subsequent history of the Swedes on the Delaware, are Thomas Campanius, grandson of the Rev. John Campanius, who came over as chaplain with Governor Printz, in 1642; the

Rev. Israel Acrelius, who was for some time provost of the Swedish Churches in America, and pastor of that at Christina; and the Rev. Andreas Rudman, of whom a full account is given in the following pages. These works were all written in the Swedish language, and for that reason their contents have been little known to the American reader. Within the last year, however, the public have been favored with a translation of Campanius, by the learned Peter S. Du Ponceau, LL.D., which he undertook at the request of the Historical Society of Pennsylvania. Of the work of Acrelius there has been no published translation; though there is a manuscript translation of it, in part, in the possession of the Historical Society of New York, which was furnished them, at their request, by the late Rev. Dr. N. Collin. The other work here referred to, that of the Rev. Mr. Rudman, is in manuscript,* and belongs to the library of the Wicaco Church. Of this also there is a manuscript translation, in part, by Dr. Collin. Acrelius refers in his work to this manuscript of Mr. Rudman, and appears to have drawn liberally from it. It has furnished to the compiler of these annals most of what, in the following pages, he offers to the public. The only originality he claims for the

* This work is entitled "Transactions relative to the Congregation at Wicaco, collected from some writings and verbal narratives."

work is, in generally presenting the facts which are detailed in his own language.

These annals are given to the public, not as a *full* account of all that has been written concerning the Swedes in America, but as presenting the most striking facts in their history, or such as the author thought would most interest his readers. He has little idea that they will be much read beyond the Swedish portion of the community, or the many descendants of those of whose early history they treat. To such he hopes the work will not be found altogether undeserving of notice. He offers it to them and to others, as a faithful narrative of past events; and such as, they will be pleased to find, represents their ancestors to view as an honest, industrious, and religious people.

It may be thought by some of the readers of these annals, that too much space is occupied in them by details relating to the Wicaco church. But it must be remembered, that this church claims a particular notice from its great antiquity, being perhaps the oldest edifice of the kind still open for public worship, and in good repair, any where to be met with in our country. The Swedish church at Wilmington (formerly Christina) was, the writer is aware, built two years before that of Wicaco, (1698,) but that, he regrets to say, has been for some time abandoned as a place of worship, and is in a state of dilapidation.* It was at Wicaco that our ancestors, in times long since departed, met from distant parts of the country to pay their weekly adorations to the God "whose never failing providence ordereth all things both in heaven and earth." In the same venerated spot many of their descendants still meet, when "the sound of the church-going bell" summons them to its services. In what Swedish bosom is not the name of Wicaco hallowed! And to whose mind will not all that relates to so ancient a church afford at least some interest.

J. C. CLAY.

Philadelphia, Nov. 28, 1834.

*Since the above was written, a legacy of some six hundred dollars has been left by a member of this old church for the purpose of putting it in a condition fit to hold worship in. The present rector, the Rev. Charles Breck, thus writes to me: "The old church is in good repair and constant use. Through the liberality of Henrietta M. Allmond, the vestry were enabled to restore and improve the old church, so that it was opened for divine service on the 21st August, 1842. In the summer of 1856, it was again thoroughly repaired, painted, etc. and the services regularly established there, through the great liberality of the lamented Alexis J. Dupont."

TABLE OF CONTENTS,

SWEDISH ANNALS.

CHAPTER I.

It is known to every reader of history that North America was discovered a short time before the year 1500. And yet it was a century afterwards before any plan for its colonization proved successful. This was no doubt owing, in a great measure, to the disturbed state of Europe at that time, when the work of the Reformation was making a rapid progress, and engaging the attention of the different powers there, either for its advancement or its suppression. Another hindrance to the earlier colonizing of this continent was, the difficulties and dangers incident to such an undertaking, and the certainty that though wealth might be the reward, the way to it must be through many perils, and the endurance of many sufferings. In the progress of time, however, there would be found some bold and adventurous enough to risk every thing for the prospect of gain; and especially, where a few had acted as pioneers, and had already triumphed over incipient difficulties. There was much, too, in the character of the age, as the Reformation advanced, or spread itself over Europe, that favored the colonization which had been so long delayed. Where the church was to be reformed, there would naturally be many opinions as to the mode of doing it, or the extent to which it ought to be done. The reformers, therefore, were not only hostile to Rome, from whom they all agreed in thinking it was right to separate, but hostile, in many instances, to one another, because they did not reform after the same manner. The consequence was, a resort to persecution, the remedy of an age not yet sufficiently enlightened to see its fallacy, for the extirpation of error, and the propagation of the truth. To those who thus suffered for their opinions, the new-discovered country presented itself as an asylum, where they might "sit under their own vine, and under their own fig tree, with none to make them afraid;" and while the thirst for gain led many to brave all the perils and privations of a new settlement, they were braved by others for the sake of liberty of conscience, and freedom from persecution.

The first permanent settlement made on the shores of this continent was in Virginia, in the year 1607, when a company of one hundred and five English adventurers came in a vessel commanded by Captain Newport, sailed up the

Powhatan or James river, built a fort, and commenced a town, which, in honor of their sovereign, they called Jamestown.

The next permanent settlement was by the Dutch, about the year 1614, on the Hudson river, discovered a few years before (1609) by Henry Hudson, an Englishman in the Dutch service, while in quest of a north-west passage to India. In settling on this noble river, the Dutch built two forts, one at Albany, and the other on Manhattan island, where the city of New York now stands. The country was called *New Netherlands*, and the settlement on Manhattan island was named *New Amsterdam*, which names they retained till the conquest of the country by the English. The governors who administered the colony during the time the Dutch had possession, were Menewe, (or Minuit,) Van Twiller, Kieft, and Stuyvesant. The Dutch authority ceased in 1664, when the whole territory became subject to the British crown.

The third permanent settlement on this continent was in New England, in the year 1620, when one hundred and one Puritans, for the better enjoyment of liberty of conscience, having sailed for Hudson's river, were taken by the master of the vessel as far north as Cape Cod, and landing, built the town of Plymouth.

In what year the first permanent settlement

was made on the shores of the Delaware, those who have treated of the early history of America seem not to have possessed the means of very accurately determining. That the Dutch were the first to settle on the eastern or Jersey shore of that river, all have agreed in admitting. And there is little less doubt that the Swedes were the first to occupy the western or Pennsylvania shore. As early as 1623 or 4, the Dutch built Fort Nassau, on the eastern shore, but soon abandoned it. Afterwards, or in the winter of 1630-31, a colony, consisting of thirty-four persons, was brought over by Captain De Vries. Returning for a short time to Holland, he left the colony under the charge of an inexperienced individual, and they were all, in 1632, exterminated by the Indians. De Vries returned in December of the same year, and entering the Delaware, found no signs of the colony he expected to meet, save their skulls and bones strewed over the face of the ground. We date, therefore, the first permanent settlement of the Dutch on the Delaware, about the year 1633. This appears to be the earliest period claimed for them by their own historians.*

It was in the reign of that illustrious king, Gustavus Adolphus, that an attempt was first made to plant a colony of Swedes in America. William Usselinx, a Hollander, had formed so

* See Moulton's History of New York.

favorable an opinion of this country, representing it as a fine, fertile land, in which all the necessaries and comforts of life were to be enjoyed in overflowing abundance, that he presented to the king the idea of a trading company, urging its establishment by such reasons as the following:—

First, That the Christian religion would by that means be planted amongst the heathen.

Second, That his Majesty's dominions would be enlarged, his treasury enriched, and the people's burdens at home diminished.

Third, That it would produce to the nation many positive advantages, and a very profitable trade; and that the Swedes possessed all the means for carrying it on with advantage.

Upon this representation, a company was established, with power to trade to Asia, Africa, and the Straits of Magellan. The king issued his proclamation, or edict, dated at Stockholm, the second of July, 1626; in which he offered to people of all conditions liberty of shares, by subscription, according to their ability, or inclinations. The proposal was received with general satisfaction. The king's mother, and Prince John Cassimir, married to his sister, the members of his majesty's council, many civil and military officers of high rank, the bishops, and other clergymen, many merchants and citizens, country gentlemen and farmers, became subscribers. Ships and all necessaries were provided. An admiral, vice-admiral, commissaries, merchants, etc., were appointed. The work was ripe for accomplishment, when the German war, and soon after, the king's death, put a stop to the proceedings, and for the present defeated the intention of sending to America a Swedish colony.

It does not appear that the idea was afterwards revived of renewing the plan of a trading company, at least upon the extensive scale at first contemplated. That of a colony was not suffered long to sleep. The Rev. Mr. Rudman, who many years afterwards bore so prominent a part in what concerned the Swedes in America, has related the following, as the manner in which a colony from Sweden was first planted here. This information he professes to have received from many individuals, particularly from one styled by him "Old Captain Israel Helms."

"Before," says he, "the Swedes came into the river, some Hollanders were here. They had a fort on the eastern shore, at the place now called Gloucester, which the Indians named Hermaomissing. This they named Fort Nassau. The commander of it was Menewe. Quarreling with the people, he left them, and returned to Holland. He was there impeached, tried, and dismissed from his office. Profiting by his knowledge of the country, he went to Sweden, and informed some of the principal gentlemen, that the Dutch had settled on the east side of the Delaware, but that the whole of the western side was unoccupied, except by the Indians. He urged to a settlement there, offering to conduct the enterprise. The project was well received, and, in particular, was favored by the prime minister, Count Oxenstiern. He laid before the Queen, Christina, the plan of a colony. She was well pleased with it, and gave (1636-7) her orders for the execution. A ship called the Key of Calmar, was fitted out from Gottenburg. Menewe was appointed commander of the colony. They arrived safely, obtained from the Indians a grant of land on the river, from the mouth of it, or Cape Henlopen, to the falls,* and there fixed stakes and marks. The old people informed me, that they often had seen these. The purchase was formally stated in writings, under which the Indians put their marks. The document was sent to Sweden and preserved in the archives, when I was at Stockholm.

"The people settled on the creek still called Christina, and erected a fort at the mouth of it; naming both in honor of their queen. Magnus Kling, their surveyor, formed a map of the country, with all its creeks and streams. This I also saw in the archives before my de-

* Trenton falls.

parture; and Mr. Auren made a small copy of it, which we brought with us. Menewe did not disturb the Dutch on the other side. He died; and Peter Hollendare succeeded him. After ruling the colony for eighteen months, he returned to Sweden, and became commander of the naval arsenal at Stockholm."*

It has been remarked by Dr. Collin, who seems to have made himself familiar with all the Swedish works that could throw any light on the first settlement of the Swedes in America, that the ship Key of Calmar, was accompanied by a smaller vessel, called Bird Grip, (Griffin,) carrying, like the other, people, provisions, ammunition, and commodities for trade

* The only inaccuracy in the above statement, appears to be in the declaration, that Peter Menewe (or Minuit according to the orthography of some) had been the commander of Fort Nassau before his return to Holland. He was in fact the first governor of New Amsterdam, (now New York.) What led to his removal from that station is not accurately known. When first appointed, and for some time afterwards, he appears to have given satisfaction to those by whom he was employed. But upon the arrival of Van Twiller, who had been sent over on business relating to the concerns of the company, dissatisfaction towards Menewe soon began to show itself, and being displaced, Van Twiller was appointed to succeed him. Mr. Rudman, it must be remembered, came to America about sixty years after the first arrival of the Swedes. Drawing, as he did, much of his information of the circumstances connected with their settlement here from traditionary sources, it was easy to substitute Fort Nassau for Fort Amsterdam, as the place of which Menewe had been the commander.

with the Indians. The time, the Doctor thinks, of this first arrival is not certainly known, but supposes it must have been in 1636 or 7, "because," says he, "the fort on Christina creek was begun early in 1638,* as appears by the protest against it by Wilhelm Kieft, the Dutch commander at New York, to Menewe, dated 6th of May in that year.

* Campanius has mentioned the year 1631 as that in which Fort Christina was built. And he has been followed in this by Smith, in his History of New Jersey, p. 22, and by Holmes in his American Annals, sub ann. 1631; who, without due examination, have fixed on this as the year when the Swedes first landed in Pennsylvania. It is only necessary to look at one fact, to show that this opinion is founded in error. It is generally admitted that the Swedes came here in the reign of their Queen Christina. It is said that Menewe "laid before *Queen Christina* the plan of a colony," etc. And the first fort built was named *after the queen*. Now Christina was not queen in 1631, nor for some time afterwards, her father Gustavus Adolphus having lost his life in the battle of Lutzen, in November 1632.

The Swedes also found the Dutch here, or on the eastern side of the river. But the Dutch had no fixed settlement here until after 1632. It must have been, therefore, after this period that the Swedes came over. How soon after is not accurately known. The remonstrance of Governor Kieft, against the building of their first fort, seems to determine it in favor of the year 1637. It was certainly not later than 1638; and as the building of a fort was, no doubt, their first undertaking after their arrival, it is not probable it was earlier than 1636. It is the opinion of Acrelius, that the originial Swedish colony came over in 1638. And the Encyclop. Americana, guided, perhaps, by his authority, has, under the article Pennsylvania, fixed on the same year for their arrival.

After the return of Hollendare to Sweden, John Printz, a lieutenant colonel in the army, was sent over as governor. He came in the year 1642, in the ship Fame. Two other ships of war called Svan (Swan) and Charitas being in company. With him came the Rev. John Campanius, as chaplain of the colony, who has left behind him a very minute account of the voyage, which the reader may see in the "Description of the Province of New Sweden," published many years afterwards by his grandson, Thomas Campanius Holm; the latter name having been added because of Stockholm being the place of his residence.

The instructions of Governor Printz, dated Stockholm, August 15, 1642, contain twenty-eight articles, embracing his duties in relation —first, to the Swedes—secondly, to the Europeans living in their vicinity—and thirdly, to the Indians. Of these instructions the following is a compendious view. In relation to the Swedes, he was to promote by the most zealous endeavors, a sincere piety, in all respects, towards Almighty God; to maintain the public worship, conformably to the doctrines and rites of the national church; to support a proper ecclesiastical discipline; to urge instruction and virtuous education of the young; to administer justice according to the Swedish laws; to preserve, as far as practicable, the manners and customs of Sweden; to promote diligently all profitable branches of industry—such as the culture of grain—the procuring of good breeds of cattle, in addition to those sent from Sweden—the raising of tobacco as an article of export to the mother country—trafficking with the Indians for peltry—searching for metals and minerals in different parts—looking after valuable kinds of wood—ascertaining what kinds of mulberry trees are best suited for the silk worm—what is the character of the native grapes, and their suitableness for wine—and whether whale and other fisheries may be carried on with advantage, etc., etc.

Secondly, with respect to the Dutch and English in their vicinity; with the first named he was to cultivate a friendly intercourse, but positively to deny their pretended right to any part of the land on the west side of the river, purchased by the Swedes from the Indians, and to prohibit Swedish vessels from passing their fort, Nassau: and he was authorised, if all friendly negotiation proved fruitless, to repel force by force. Those Dutch families who had settled on the west side, under allegiance to the crown of Sweden, were to retain the granted privileges, but to be advised and persuaded to remove further down from the vicinity of Christina Fort, yet not driven away if anxious to remain. The governor was to continue the friendly commercial intercourse with the English in Virginia, then comprehending Maryland, which had already been begun, by supplying their colony with grain, cattle, and other useful articles. Some English families, embracing about sixty persons, having settled in the preceding year, (1641,) on Ferken's creek, (now Salem,) and the agents of the company having, as her majesty's subjects, bought from the Indian owners the whole district from Cape May to Racoon creek, in order to unite these English with the Swedes, the governor was to act faithfully and kindly towards them. And as these English expected soon, by further arrivals to increase their number to several hundred; and seemed also willing to be subjects of the Swedish government, he was to receive them under allegiance, though not without endeavoring by gentle means, to effect their removal.

Thirdly, Respecting the Indians; the governor was directed to confirm, immediately after his arrival, the treaty with that people, by which they had conveyed to the Swedes the western shore of the Delaware, from Cape Henlopen to the Falls of Sanhickan (Trenton,) and as much inland as gradually should be wanted. Also, to ratify the bargain for land on the east side above mentioned; and in these and future purchases, to regard them as the rightful owners of the country. He was to treat all the neighboring tribes in the most equitable and humane manner, so that no injury, by violence or otherwise, should be done to them by any of his people. He had also in charge to accomplish, as far as practicable, the embracing of Christianity by them, and their adoption of the manners and customs of civilized life.

Governor Printz chose Tinicum, then called Tenackongh, and Tutaenungh, for his residence. He erected a fort on the shore, to which he gave the name of New Gottenburg. A decent church was also built there of wood, which was consecrated by Campanius, Sept. 4, 1646. The trade of the Swedes being interfered with by the Dutch, the fort at Elsingborough, called by the Swedes Helsingborg, was erected by Printz, to command the river, but became untenable from the great multitude of musquitoes, and was nicknamed Myggenborg, or Mosquito Fort. Upon the erection of this fort, the Dutch left Fort Nassau, opposite Tinicum, and took possession of Sandhuken (now New Castle) on the west side, where they built Fort Cassimir. The governor protested against it, as encroaching on Swedish ground, but had not sufficient force to prevent it. He made proper representations to his government on the subject, and requested a speedy reinforcement; but weary with the delay, and apprehensive of violence from the Dutch, from the hostile disposition manifested by them, and their near neighborhood,* he resolved on re-

* Five miles from Fort Christina.

turning to Sweden, and in 1652 left the country, after a residence in it of ten years. He had become unpopular by the exercise of a too rigid authority.

In the mean time, John Claudius Rising had been sent from the mother country as commissioner and assistant to governor Printz. On his arrival, the governor had already sailed for Sweden, and had left his son-in-law, Mr. John Pappegoia, as deputy-governor in his place. He also, two years afterwards, returned to his native country, and left the government in the hands of Mr. Rising. With this last named gentleman came Peter Lindstrom, engineer and surveyor-general, with several military officers and other agents. Mr. Rising immediately offered to the English and Dutch, and also to the Indians, a renewal of the former friendship. During the administration of Printz, other vessels, besides those above mentioned, arrived at different times, from the mother country. These were, the Black Cat, with ammunition and goods for the Indians—the Swan, a second time, with people, in 1647; and afterwards the Key and the Lamb.

Soon after Mr. Rising became governor, he invited ten of the Indian Chiefs to a friendly conference. It was held at Tinicum, on the 17th of June 1654. He saluted them, from the Swedish Queen, with assurances of her favor, put them in mind of the purchase of the lands already made, and requested a continuation of their friendship. He distributed various presents among them, and gave a good entertainment to them and their company. They were much pleased, and assured him of a faithful affection. Mr. Campanius has given a very particular account of this conference, in which he represents one of their chiefs, named Naaman, as making a speech, in the course of which "he rebuked the rest for having spoken evil of the Swedes, and done them an injury, hoping they would do so no more, for that the Swedes were very good people." He also observed that "the Swedes and the Indians had been as one body and one heart, and that thenceforward they should be as one head, at the same time making a motion as if he were tying a strong knot; and then made this comparison, that as the calabash was round without any crack, so they should be a compact body without any fissure."

Campanius represents the Indians as having been frequent visitors at his grandfather's house. In the conversations he there had with them, we are told, "he generally succeeded in making them understand that there was one Lord God; that he was self-existent, one and in three persons; how the same God made the world from nothing, and created man from whom all other men had sprung; how Adam afterwards, by his disobedience, had sinned against his Creator, and involved in the penalty of that sin all his descendants; how God sent upon earth his only Son, Jesus Christ, who was born of the Virgin Mary, for the redemption and salvation of Mankind; how he died upon the cross, and was raised again the third day; and lastly, how after forty days he ascended to heaven, whence he will return at a future day to judge the quick and the dead, etc." The Indians took so much interest in these instructions, and seemed so well disposed to embrace the Christian religion, that Mr. Campanius was induced to learn their language, that he might the more effectually bring them acquainted with these great truths. He translated the catechism into their language; and, if he did not convert many of them to the Christian faith, they at least acquired so much knowledge of it, as to be led to see and admire its great beauty and excellency.

The above facts suggest the remark, that the Swedes may claim the honor of having been the first missionaries among the Indians, at least in Pennsylvania; and that, perhaps, the very first work translated into the Indian language in America, was the translation of Luther's Catechism, by Campanius.

CHAPTER II.

Notwithstanding Governor Rising's disposition to live upon good terms with his Dutch neighbors, the Swedes were soured by the encroachments they had made upon their territory, in building a fort at Sandhuken, or Newcastle; and finding remonstrance useless, soon came to the determination to drive the Dutch back to the eastern side of the river. They accordingly, in the year 1654, took Fort Cassimir by storm, and expelled the Dutch; after which, the fortifications were greatly strengthened and improved by the engineer, P. Lindstrom, and it was named *Trefalldigheet*, or Trinity Fort.

The Dutch had too good an opinion of their own numbers and prowess, not to feel disposed to retaliate on the Swedes the injury they had received in the loss of their fort. Yet they went to work with caution, resolving, when they gave the blow, to make it the more felt from its being sudden and unexpected. There seems to have been a want of good faith, or at least the practice of some deception on the part of the Dutch, as we are told by Campanius that "the differences appeared to have been amicably settled in the year 1654, between the Swedish governor John Rising, and the Dutch governor Peter Stuyvesant." This amicable settlement seems to have been only a cloak to preparations for more effectual hostility; for "the next year, on the 30th of August, the Dutch sailed from Manhattan, or New Amsterdam, (now New York,) with seven ships, and six or seven hundred men, under the command of the said Stuyvesant; and fell unawares on the Swedish settlements." Assailed under such circumstances, and by such a force, resistance was of little avail. One Swedish fort after another fell into the hands of the invaders, who "laid waste the houses and plantations, killing the cattle, and plundering the inhabitants of every thing they could lay their hands on." The officers and principal people were made prisoners, and carried to New Amsterdam, while the Dutch retained possession of the country.

That the Swedes were in a state so unprepared for the attack made upon them by the Dutch, was owing to the mother country being but little able to assist them, on account of the expensive wars in which she was engaged at home. The Dutch were fully aware that all the reliance of the Swedes was on their own resources; and while they looked to this for an easy conquest of their territory, no doubt calculated also that here they would find subsequent impunity. In justification of the hostility he had committed, Stuveysant pretended that what he had done was in the name of the West India Company of Amsterdam, and that he had not conquered a territory of the Swedish crown, but that of a company. Yet he very well knew that these people were living under the laws of Sweden, and under the guardianship of the Swedish crown; and that, consequently, any insult or injury offered to them, was an offence against the government under whose protection they were placed.

In 1656, or about a year after the conquest by the Dutch, a Swedish ship called Mercurius, arrived in the river. This the Dutch wished to prevent going up; but the Indians, who loved the Swedes, interfered in their behalf, and in defiance of the others conveyed the ship by their fort. "Among the passengers in this vessel," says Mr. Rudman, "was Andrew Bengtson, sen.* yet living, who, this 6th day of April, 1703, gives me this verbal account." As it was not in the power of the mother country, on account of the wars in which she was engaged, to prevent the conquest of New Sweden by the Dutch, so, for the same reason, was she unable to carry into effect her disposition to recover what she had thus lost. It was not long, however, before the face of things here was entirely changed; and they who had dispossessed the Swedes, by the exercise of a high-

* His descendants (the Bankson family) are still living in Philadelphia.

handed authority, were themselves dispossessed by the English, who claimed the right of first discovery to most of the North American continent. It was in 1664 that a British force arrived from England, and, attacking the Dutch in their strong hold at New York, soon put an end to their authority, bringing them and the Swedes under allegiance to the British crown.

The manner in which Pennsylvania became settled by the English is well known. The large territory comprehended under this name, was granted by Charles II. to William Penn, in compensation of a large sum owed by the government to his father, Admiral Penn, Penn came over in 1682, and founded the city of Philadelphia. The Swedes, who were owners of the soil, opposed the undertaking, but by kind promises and other means were, after a while, induced to agree to it. "The city," Mr. Rudman says, "had a poor beginning, but attained admirable improvement in twenty years."* Penn offered the Swedes a portion of land, where they might live together, and enjoy their own customs; but they preferred remaining as they were, which their descendants, in Rudman's time, seem bitterly to have regretted.

About this time an imposter, who bore the

* About the time of Mr. Rudman's arrival, in 1697, Philadelphia and New York were spoken of as *clever little towns*.

name of Koenigsmark, arrived among the Swedes, and having gained many adherents, especially among the Finns, raised a sedition, though with what object does not appear. This man was apprehended, branded, and exiled. His followers were fined, and some lost their land. The disturbances occasioned in this manner seem to have lessened the good opinion Penn had formed of the Swedes. He continued, however, his good offices towards them; and having before this returned to England, sent them books and catechisms, and a folio Bible for their church.

In a letter written by William Penn to England the year after his arrival, he thus speaks of the first settlers of the country: "The first planters in these parts were the Dutch, and soon after them the Swedes and Finns. The Dutch applied themselves to traffic, the Swedes and Finns to husbandry. The Dutch have a meeting place for religious worship at Newcastle, and the Swedes one at Christina, one at Tinicum, and one at Wicaco, within half a mile of this town. The Swedes inhabit the freshes of the River Delaware. There is no need of giving any description of them, who are better known in England than here; but they are a plain, strong, industrious people, yet have made no great progress in the culture or propagation of fruit trees, as if they desired rather to have enough than plenty or traffic. But I presume the Indians made them the more careless, by furnishing them with the means of profit, to wit, skins and furs for rum, and such strong liquors. They kindly received me, as well as the English, who were few before the people concerned with me came among them. I must needs commend their respect to authority, and kind behavior to the English. They do not degenerate from the old friendship between both kingdoms. As they are a people proper and strong of body, so have they fine children, and almost every house full; rare to find one of them without three or four boys, and as many girls: some six, seven, and eight sons. And I must do them the justice to say, I see few young men more sober and industrious."*

It was a feature deserving of notice in the character of the early Swedes inhabiting this country, as will more fully appear in the sequel of these annals, that in the attention they paid to other concerns and interests, they never appear to have lost sight of those relating to God, and the worship due to him. As a religious people they are presented to us in a most favorable light, and may well be held up as an example for the imitation of their numerous descendants still occupying the soil so long ago inhabited by their ancestors. In coming to this new country, they did not forget that their residence in it was to be but for a season, and

* Clarkson's Life of W. Penn, vol. i. p. 309.

that there was another, and a heavenly country for which it was their duty to make preparation. They accordingly brought with them the ministers of religion, to instruct them and their children in the knowledge of things divine. In the time of Menewe there was a clergyman here of the name of Reorus Torkillus, who came perhaps with the first colony, as he died in 1643, aged thirty-five years. The Rev. John Campanius, as we have seen, came over in 1642. He returned to Sweden in 1648, became rector of a considerable parish, and lived to the age of eighty-two years. Laurence Lock and Israel Holg came while Printz was governor. A chaplain came with Rising, and went home after the conquest by the Dutch. A clergyman also arrived in the same ship with Mr. Bengtson in 1656, but did not remain long. Lock continued in the country, having charge of the church at Tinicum and Christina, and died in the year 1688. From him many families descended, and several are yet living in West Jersey, near the Delaware. They were among the best members of Racoon church.

As long as the Swedes were in possession of authority here, and lived under their own laws, there appears to have been frequent intercourse between them and the mother country; at least frequent for that time, when a voyage across the Atlantic was considered as formidable an undertaking as one to China is at the present day. But when their colonial character ceased, and the Dutch, and afterwards the English, became masters of the soil, the intercourse between them and their friends at home, was in a short time, entirely dropped, and they were left to get along in the best way they could. In matters relating to their temporal concerns, the stood in need of little assistance. But for a supply of clergymen they were entirely dependent on the mother country; and soon felt how much they were likely to suffer, in this respect, from the interruption that had taken place to the intercourse between them and their native land. For many years the Rev. Mr. Lock was the only clergyman they had. As already remarked, he preached in the lower parishes. The upper inhabitants had, by order of government, erected a block house at Wicaco, for defence against the Indians. As the distance to Tinicum rendered an attendance at public worship there very inconvenient, this block-house was converted into a church. To get a place of worship was easier than to find a clergyman to occupy it. They applied, for this purpose, to the Rev. Jacob Fabritius, of New York, who accepted a call to Wicaco, where he preached his first sermon on Trinity Sunday,* in the year 1677.†

* Mr. Fabritius preached in the Dutch language, which the Swedes, from the intercourse they had with that people, and the close affinity between the two languages, well understood.

† See Appendix A.

Mr. Fabritius preached for the Swedes for a period of fourteen years, though for nine years of that time he was entirely blind. Being at last disabled from further service through the infirmities of old age, the people were under serious apprehensions lest they should be left without a minister. To prevent so great an evil, they had, while Mr. F. was yet able to officiate, twice written to Sweden, representing their want of a pastor. These letters, it appears, were never received. Discouraged by this failure, they applied to the Lutheran Consistory at Amsterdam, to procure for them a minister, by ordaining and sending them some Swedish student of theology who might be in that city; or, if no such person could be obtained, to correspond in their behalf with some ecclesiastical body in Sweden. This letter was written in 1691.*

The reason of this application of the Swedes to Holland rather than to England, was, their ignorance of the English language, and the little intercourse they had had with the latter nation; as well as the greater probability, as they thought, of getting a Swedish minister through the former channel than the latter. Here again, however, they were destined to meet with disappointment. No preacher came, and the prospect became very dark and gloomy. The Rev.

* See Appendix B.

Mr. Lock had died in 1688, and Mr. Fabritius four or five years afterwards, so that they were now entirely without a clergyman. In this extremity they resolved still to keep their churches open, and appointed two worthy and pious men to perform for them the office of Lay readers; who, besides the prayers and psalms, read homilies or sermons. The person who officiated in this capacity at Wicaco was Mr. Andrew Bengtsen or Bankson; and at Christina they had Mr. Charles Christopher Springer.*

* This Mr. Springer wrote the letter to Thelin, presently to come under our notice. He was a native Swede, and had come to America by a remarkable providence. He was in the family of the Swedish ambassador in London. Going home one evening in a post-chaise, he was seized, and carried on board of a merchant vessel, in the Thames, bound to Virginia. He was there sold as a servant for five years. When free, he went to the Swedes, and by his capacity and virtue acquired such an influence as to be appointed justice of the peace in the district of Christina. He was afterwards, for many years, a useful member of that church.

CHAPTER III.

We here arrive at a most interesting part of our narrative. The reader has observed with what a holy and praise-worthy zeal the attention of the first settlers on this soil was directed to the introduction and continuance among them of the blessings of a preached Gospel; he has seen that, after succeeding in this for a period of rather more than fifty years, they found all efforts to have the vacant congregations supplied with other clergymen, to administer to them and their children the ordinances of the church, ending in utter disappointment, and a dark cloud resting on the future. Now who that has observed the usual dealings of God's providence in behalf of his people, where they have been thrown into difficulties such as the present, is not led to expect his interposition in behalf of these pious Swedes, thus striving to secure to themselves and their posterity the privileges and blessings of the ministry of his church? It is when human aid fails, that divine assistance is not only most needed, but is most looked for, and its exercise is most apt to strike the eye of the observer. We know there are some disposed to deny this doctrine of a superintending providence, and to laugh at the idea of God interposing in the affairs of men. But what will not man deny when acting under the impulses of "an evil heart of unbelief?" It is true, God acts through the instrumentality of human means; as when he made use of the brethren of Joseph for the accomplishment of those wonderful designs of his providence brought about by the residence of the latter in Egypt. But his controlling influence is not the less seen and felt in the world because he makes use of subordinate agents for the accomplishment of his purposes. Let the means be what they may, we are sure of the truth of the doctrine; as every one must be sure of it who receives the scriptural declaration that "God ruleth in the armies of heaven, and among the inhabitants of the earth."

With regard to the Swedes, in the crisis of their affairs at which we have arrived, while all was dark before them, He, "without whom not even a sparrow falleth to the ground," was preparing the way for a supply of their spiritual wants, and in a short time afforded them the deliverance they had been seeking. About the time of which we are writing, a person of the name of Andrew Printz, a nephew, as he said, of Governor Printz, had come over in an English vessel to the Delaware, and being himself a Swede, had become acquainted with his countrymen here, by whom he had been cordially received. Meeting, on his return to Sweden, with John Thelin, postmaster at Gottenburg, he mentioned to that gentleman his having met, across the Atlantic, with some of their countrymen, whose condition he represented as very comfortable in things temporal, but very forlorn and destitute in a spiritual point of view. This pious man was at once interested in their behalf, and he resolved to lay their case before the king, Charles XI. This led to the following letter, which was addressed by Mr. Thelin to the Swedes on the Delaware.

" *Hon. Friends and Countrymen,*

" The occasion which leads me to write to you is, that when last year I was at Stockholm I met with one Andrew Printz, who, I found, had been in an English vessel to the West Indies. Upon my questioning him whether he had a prosperous voyage, he told me he had found there a good land, and had also met with some old Swedes in good prosperity, who had greatly rejoiced to see one from their native country, and had inquired who was now the reigning king of Sweden: and that you, good friends, had confidence in his majesty that if he were made acquainted with your want of ministers and godly books, he would provide for your necessities. When he had related such things to me, I took greatly, as did others, your condition to heart; and having good friends at his majesty's court, I related these things to an honorable lord, who again mentioned them to his majesty. Whereupon his majesty took therein a special and particular interest, and resolved that he would send unto you not only ministers, but also all sorts of godly books; and would willingly have used for an agent in accomplishing these purposes the same man who had related these things. But the Lord knoweth what became of that man; for he could not be seen nor heard of afterwards. Therefore I now do take the boldness upon me, being acquainted with an elderly woman here, who says she has a brother living among you, Peter Gunnarson Rambo, through whom this letter may be received, that I may know from you the truth of what has been related, and in what way such ministers may be sent to you; desiring that you would let it be distinctly known of what it is you are in need.

"The aforesaid person has told me that you live comfortably, and in a loving manner one with another, and that you use the old Swedish way in every thing, which it has much pleased his majesty to hear. And surely the great and special care which his majesty taketh for you should rejoice our hearts; who being in close friendship and alliance with his most excellent majesty of England, your desires may be the more readily carried into effect. Indeed, this work doth certainly come and spring from the Almighty God, in whose hands are the hearts of kings, so that you may speedily send your answer, that it may be for your soul's health and happiness. And we desire to know the number of ministers and books which you desire to have; and also how many you are in number, and how many churches you have. About eight or ten years ago, the governor, William Penn, petitioned the Swedish Ambassador at London for ministers and books for you; but for some cause or other, the request was not carried into effect. Be not negligent in the things which belong to your everlasting happiness; for you may certainly see that the Great God doth as soon help through friends that are humble as through those that are great and powerful. I commend you to the holy protection of Almighty God, both in soul and body. I shall expect to hear from you by the first opportunity that may offer, and remain your most loving friend and servant.

JEAN THELIN

"Gottenburg, 16th Nov. 1692.

"P. S. I send a duplicate of this letter, that you may be the more certain of receiving it."

The receipt of this letter caused great joy to the Swedes, who determined on a speedy answer. But as they were now living under the laws of England, they deemed it prudent and advisable to lay the whole matter before the English governor, William Markham. The governor expressed himself much gratified, and wished them not to delay answering the letter. He also offered to write in their behalf to the Proprietor, William Penn, and to Lejoncrona, the Swedish minister in London. With these favorable auspices, Charles Springer wrote for the Swedes their answer to Mr. Thelin's letter. Upon the receipt of it in Sweden, it was copied by many persons, and drew tears from the eyes of many who heard its contents. It was dated May 31, 1693, and was as follows:

"Honored, loving, and much respected friend, John Thelin, his majesty's loyal subject, and Postmaster at Gottenburg,

"Your unexpected and welcome letter, dated Gottenburg, 16th Nov. 1692, came to hand the 23d of May, 1693, and made us heartily rejoice that it hath pleased Almighty God, through that young man Andrew Printz, to make known our condition to our friends in Sweden. We rejoice that his majesty doth still bear unto us a tender and a christian care. Therefore do we heartily desire, since it hath pleased his majesty graciously to regard our wants, that there may be sent unto us two Swedish ministers, who are well learned in the Holy Scriptures, and who may be able to defend them an d us against all false opposers; so that we may preserve our true Lutheran faith, which, if called to suffer for our faith, we are ready to seal with our blood. We also request that those ministers may be men of good moral lives and characters;

so that they may instruct our youth by their example, and lead them into a pious and virtuous way of life.

"Further, it is our humble desire that you would be pleased to send us three books of sermons, twelve bibles, forty-two psalm books, one hundred tracts, with two hundred catechisms, and as many primers; for which, when received, we promise punctual payment at such place as you may think fit to order. We do promise also a proper maintenance to the ministers that may be sent to us; and when this our letter is gone, it is our intention to buy a piece of land, that shall belong to the church, and upon which the ministers may live.

"As to what concerns our situation in this country, we are for the most part husbandmen. We plough and sow, and till the ground; and as to our meat and drink, we live according to the old Swedish custom. This country is very rich and fruitful, and here grow all sorts of grain in great plenty, so that we are richly supplied with meat and drink; and we send out yearly to our neighbors on this continent and the neigboring islands, bread, grain, flour and oil. We have here also, all sorts of beasts, fowls, and fishes. Our wives and daughters employ themselvos in spinning wool and flax, and many of them in weaving; so that we have great reason to thank the Almighty for his manifold mercies and benefits. God grant that we may also have good shepherds, to feed us with his holy word and sacraments. We live also in peace and friendship with one another; and the Indians have not molested us for many years.

"Further, since this country has ceased to be under the government of Sweden, we are bound to acknowledge and declare, for the sake of truth, that we have been well and kindly treated, as well by the Dntch, as by his majesty, the King of England, our gracious sovereign: on the other hand, we, the Swedes, have been and still are true and faithful to him in words and in deeds. We have always had over us good and gracious magistrates; and we live with one another in peace and quietness. So that we desire, as soon as this our letter comes to hand, that a speedy attention may be paid to our request; for we believe that God has certainly his hand in this christian work, and pray that he may bring it to a happy termination."

With this letter was sent a separate account of all the people, mentioning the heads of families, and the number of persons in each, and a mark to distinguish those who were born in Sweden.* It was thus headed—"An accurate list of all the men, women, and children now found living in New Sweden, at present Pennsylvania, on the river Delaware." Among those

* See Appendix C.

born in Sweden, Peter Rambo and Andrew Bonde (now Boon) had been in the country fifty-four years.

The above letter to John Thelin was signed by thirty persons. When received by that gentleman, it was forwarded to the court. At a period when there was so little intercourse between this country and Europe, and scarcely any that was direct between here and Sweden, it took a long time for an interchange of letters between the Swedes of the mother country and those of Pennsylvania. This may explain the long interval that elapsed between the writing of the above letter, in May, 1693, and the date (Feb. 7, 1696) of the first measures taken in Sweden towards furnishing the desired spiritual relief. According to Campanius, there was no delay in taking those measures; and he says, "as soon as the letter arrived at Stockholm, his majesty, Charles XI. of glorious memory, in order to promote the preservation of our holy religion among this small number of settlers in America, wrote on the subject to the late Dr. Olaus Suebilius, Archbishop of Upsal."

This interesting letter we here lay before the reader:

"Charles, by the grace of God, king of Sweden, etc., etc.

"Our faithful and well-beloved Archbishop: We send you herewith a letter from the Swedish colony on the river Delaware, to John Thelin, the postmaster at Gottenburg, and by him delivered to our department of state. From which we have seen, with great pleasure, that this people have a very pious zeal for the preservation to themselves and their children, of the pure evangelical religion. We are by this moved to grant them aid, and to favor their petition for obtaining two clergymen It is, therefore, our pleasure that you will carefully select for them such good and learned pastors as they desire to have; and it is our will that, as soon as they shall be ready for their voyage, they be provided with a passage, and the necessary funds to defray their expenses. You will also procure the bibles, homilies, common-prayer and hymn-books, catechisms, primers, and spiritual treatises which are desired; so that the ministers may take these books along with them, which we will present free of expense. We are persuaded that you will be solicitous to procure faithful laborers in this vineyard of the Lord. In so doing you will promote the glory of God, and also give us great satisfaction. We commend you kindly to Almighty God. Given at Stockholm, the 18th of February, 1696.

CHARLES.

"*By the King. C. PIPER.*"

On the receipt of this letter from his majesty, the Archbishop laid the matter before the consistory and consulted the members of it. "He afterwards," says the Rev. Mr. Rudman, "called me, without any previous notice, and by many pathetic motives urged my acceptance of this mission. I desired some days for consideration, and agreed. But, foreseeing the necessary troubles of this enterprise, I requested of him to lay before the king my humble petition for leave to return, in due time, and promotion at home. He did so, and received the following answer:

"'Charles, by the Grace of God, &c. Trusty and well-beloved Archbishop: We have received your letter, dated the 21st inst., in which you promise to procure, according to our mandate, pious and learned clergymen, for preaching the pure evangelical religion to the Swedish people in America. We grant your request in their behalf, that they may have permission to return after some years, and obtain suitable preferment; as it would otherwise be a great hardship to leave their native country. You will, therefore, assure them of this our gracious intention. Given at Stockholm, the 22d of February, 1696.

CHARLES.

"'*By the King. C. PIPER.*'"

CHAPTER IV.

The king having thus given his consent that the ministers to be sent to America, should, in due time, if they desired it, be permitted to return to their native land, the Rev. Mr. Rudman obtained leave to choose a suitable colleague. Several persons were thought of, but at the suggestion of Professor Jesper Swedberg, the Rev. Eric Biork, a native of the province of Westmanland, was selected as highly qualified for this important work. The king saw fit to appoint a third clergyman to accompany the other two, and fixed on the Rev. Jonas Auren, of the province of Wermeland. He was commissioned to view the country, and in a short time to return and make his report. These two were accordingly ordained at Upsal. The king provided for them the necessary outfit; and having taken leave of their friends and relatives, they felt anxious to be gone, but were for a while detained by the printer not being ready with the Indian catechisms.

Before their departure, the following royal mandate was issued:—"It is the gracious will of his majesty, that the three clergymen, Andrew Rudman, Eric Biork, and Jonas Auren, chosen by the Archbishop of Upsal, for the Swedish congregations in America, shall take with them the religious books, mentioned in the annexed catalogue, as a donation from the king, with a declaration of his great satisfaction in their prosperity, and their faithful constancy in the pure evangelical religion. Given at Stockholm, the 15th of July, 1696.

CHARLES."

The books sent were the following:

30 Bibles; 10 printed by Vankis and 20 by Keiser.
6 Books of Homilies; 2 Cabinets of Treasures; 2 of Moellers; 2 of Lutheman's.
150 Manuals.
100 Religious treatises of different kinds, viz: 12 by Kellingius; Garden of Paradise; Atlice, etc.
100 Books of Common Prayer and Hymns.
2 Ecclesiastical Acts.
2 Church Regulations.
100 Catechisms of Archbishop Suebilius.
300 Compends of do. do.
400 Primers.
500 Catechisms in the Indian language.

The king appropriated three thousand dollars for the expenses of the missionaries; and the director of the custom house was appointed to provide a good ship for their passage. The ship Palmboom, Captain Hogen, was selected for the purpose. The three clergymen then waited on the king, with the most respectful and affectionate thanks for his favors. He gave them his hand, and said, "Go now, in the name of the Lord, to the place whither I send you. God be with you, and prosper your undertaking. If any opposition or injury befal you, return, and I will remember you." Then addressing Mr. Auren, in whose father's house he had often been, he said, "you will soon come back; salute your parents." Auren went to Gottenburg to take leave of his friends, intending to sail from that port, and meet his colleagues in London. The Rev. Messrs. Rudman and Biork embarked on the 4th of August, 1696.

After encountering a violent storm in the North Sea, and being in danger, in the English Channel, of losing the ship on a shoal called the Onion, on which the vessel struck several times, they arrived safely in London on the 10th of October. They had letters to the court requesting permission to proceed to America. There was some hesitation in granting such permission, but it was after a while obtained. This delay proved in the end of advantage to the missionaries. They had engaged their passage in the ship Happy Union, but being detained in the manner just mentioned, that vessel was obliged to sail without them. This ship was overtaken by a storm, and after losing sails, masts, and rudder, with difficulty reached a port in Portugal, and did not arrive in America until a year after the landing there of the missionaries. The first opportunity these had of leaving England was on the 4th of February, 1697, in the ship Jeffris, Captain Cooper. After a long detention in the Eglish Channel, waiting for their convoy, they put to sea, and in ten weeks reached the coast of Virginia. Entering the Chesapeake Bay they proceeded up to Annapolis in Maryland, where lived the governor of that province, Francis Nicholson, who received them with the greatest hospitality and kindness. After remaining there two weeks, they took a shallop, and on the 24th of June, being St. John's day, arrived in Elk river, and landing, found some of their countrymen residing there. These immediately sent word of the circumstance to the Swedes in Pennsylvania, who, going thither, received them with tears of joy, and conveyed them and their baggage to the Swedish settlement. Before mentioning what took place on their arrival there, we here give the letter addressed to the Swedes in America by the archbishop of Upsal.

"To the respectable Swedish congregations in America, grace, peace, and blessing from God the Father, through Jesus Christ.

"Whereas, beloved friends, you have, with a laudable zeal for the preservation of the pure evangelical religion, and by it the promotion of your spiritual welfare, supplicated his majesty, my gracious king, to send over to you two pious and learned clergymen; and whereas his majesty has been pleased to grant your humble request, and has commissioned me to procure two such clergymen, I have, in obedience to his mandate, and in compliance with my official duty, selected the Rev. Andrew Rudman, Master of Philosophy, and Mr. Eric Biork; who, on examination, are found competent to the office, and who are known to be of pious and orderly character, and willing to take upon themselves this long and hazardous voyage. They are supplied by the king's royal favor, with the necessary funds for that voyage; which I wish, by God's grace, may be safe and prosperous. I therefore recommend them to you as proper teachers for the Swedish congregations. They will do their best to promote your spiritual welfare, by preaching God's word as contained in the Old and New Testaments, teaching the Apostles', Nicene and Athanasian creeds, and the true doctrines contained in the Augsburg Confession of Faith, free from all human superstition and tradition. They will administer the holy sacraments according to God's ordinances, and they will instruct your children in the catechism. They will also, it is hoped, set before you examples in all Christian graces and virtues, by a godly, sober, and irreproachable life; that they may give a good account to the Supreme Shepherd when he shall come. On your part, beloved friends, I have full confidence that you will receive these gentlemen as your true spiritual guardians, and render them all the honor and obedience due to their sacred function; also recompensing their official labors by a sufficient maintenance, according to the commandment of God, and your own promise.

"Whereupon we commend you to the protection of Almighty God, with faithful wishes of prosperity, increase in religious wisdom, and constancy in the way of salvation.

"Given under our hand and the seal of the Cathedral Consistory of Upsal, the 25th of June, 1696.

OLAUS SUEBILIUS,
Archbishop of Upsal."

As to what took place in the Swedish settlements, and in what condition the missionaries found the people, we cannot do better than lay before the reader the following extracts of letters written by the Rev. Eric Biork to the Right Rev. Superintendent, Doctor Israel Kolmodin, dated Christina Creek, 29th of October, 1697.

"I had the pleasure of writing to you on the 4th of February, to inform you that we were about to leave London. We went on board that day, but were detained some time at Deal and Portsmouth, until the convoys and the captains could be cleared; at last, on the 22d of March, we weighed anchor at Portsmouth, and having passed Plymouth, the last land that we saw on the 24th was the Lizard, and from that time we saw no land until we reached Virginia. I shall not detain you with the particulars of our voyage, which was as usual, made up of storms and fair weather, but shall at once tell you, that on the 31st of May, in the afternoon, we found ourselves in thirty-four fathoms depth, and were delighted to see land before us, which we were informed was Smith's Island. We tacked about until the 2d of June, in the morning, when we cast anchor in seven fathoms depth, with joy and gladness. We went afterwards to seek a safe harbor in James river, in which we remained some days, while the captain was making his arrangements; thence, on the 10th of June, we sailed by Maryland, Newport, Rappahannock, Potomac, Point Lookout, the first point in Maryland, and Pautuxent to a town on the river Severn, called Annapolis, where resides the governor, Francis Nicholson, and there we cast anchor, on the 19th of June. I would fain relate to you all the attention that we received from the said governor, but suffice it to say that he treated us with the greatest kindness and respect. Our gracious sovereign and his royal family were duly remembered, and had we been sent recommended to that gentleman directly from Sweden, he could not have done more for us. We remained four days in his house, during which time he did all in his power to entertain us, and show us every thing worth seeing; when at last we were obliged to go on board our ship, to continue our voyage, he took all the trouble upon himself, to see every thing properly done; and when we took leave of him, he accompanied us part of the way, gave us a sum of money, and sent two men with us, to put on board as many bottles as they could carry, filled with all kinds of liquors. The governor is a single man, looks like a brave soldier, and is greatly attached to his king, of whom he is a faithful servant. On the 23d of June we went on board with all our things; and we can never forget the captain's goodness, who carried us through such a long voyage without charging any freight or passage money. At last, with a fair wind, we sailed about seventeen English miles, to a place called Transtown,* situated on Elk river, at the distance of an English mile from our Swedish settlement, where we joyfully landed, returning thanks to God for having safely brought us through such a long voyage.

"Before we had been there a day and a night, the people flocked in great numbers to see us; they came from a distance of ten or twelve Swedish miles,† in order to conduct us to their place of meeting. They welcomed us with great joy, and would hardly believe we had arrived until they saw us. They were, indeed, in great want of spiritual assistance; for at the

* Probably Frenchtown.

† A Swedish mile is equal to 6⅔ English miles.

same time that I, though unworthy, was appointed to this high office, they were deprived by death of their venerable teacher, the Rev. Jacob Fabritius; and since that time have had nobody but their reader, Charles Christopher Springer, a plain, honest, pious man, but devoid of talents; however, by the grace of God, who can produce great things out of little ones, they did tolerably well with him, as he was very zealous, and spared no pains to promote their spiritual welfare, as I myself have always witnessed.

"On the 27th of June, we had only a small meeting of prayer and thanksgiving, at the lower congregation. On the 29th, we went up to Philadelphia, a clever little town,* and waited on the lieutenant governor, William Markham, who, when he saw our credentials, received us with great kindness.

"On the 30th of June, we visited the upper congregation at a place called Wicaco,† which is the nearest to Philadelphia, and where the

*Then about fourteen years old.

†Where the Swedish Church now stands, which was then out of town. Wicaco, otherwise spelt Wicacoa, seems to have been the Indian name given to this place. The Swedes and many others, more frequently spoke of their churches in reference to the *places* where they were situated, than their proper ecclesiastical *titles*. It was "*Wicaco* Church," not Gloria Dei; "*Christina* Church," not Trinity, by which these churches were for a long time familiarly known; and so of others.

OLD
BLOCK
HOUSE

Swedes have a church,* in which we gave them an account of our voyage and objects, beginning with their own letter to the postmaster at Gottenburg, then his royal majesty's orders given thereupon, etc. etc. We did the same thing on the 2d of July, to the lower congregation at Tranhook,† where they also have a church. On the 11th of July, I, their unworthy minister, clad in my surplice, delivered my first discourse to them in Jesus' name, on the subject of the righteousness of the Pharisees, (*de justitia Pharisæorum.*)

"And now, to say something more respecting our congregations, I must confess that they did not entirely comply with what they had promised in their letter: the reason was, that they were most uncomfortably situated, the land which led to their church being then overflowed with water, and yet they would not abandon the place until they should have ministers, to whom they could commit the work, in which, through God's grace, I have succeeded, and agreed with them to fix on a more convenient place to build a stone church, to be called Christina Church. I hope it will be done in a year, for the congregations are rich,

*This church was originally a block-house. It is not known when it was built, but was first used as a place of worship in 1677. It had loop-holes and occupied the site of the present church.

†Near Christina.

and easily persuaded by good reasons, such as I have given them. In comparing the religious situation of these people, their divine service, attention to ordinances, and instruction of their youth in the catechism, and other things, with the congregations in Sweden, I must say that these are quite irregular, and that makes us fear that we shall have great labor and difficulty; but we remember our oaths, which are always before our minds, and will endeavor to bring them as nearly as possible to the state of the congregations in Sweden. This state of things is not to be wondered at; for their ministers, particularly the last, were old and infirm, and could not pay proper attention to the education of youth; but we hope, if God grants us life, to mend these matters; so that there will be churches, dwellings, and gardens for the ministers; and that divine service will be performed, the ordinances administered, the youth taught their catechism, and regular examinations take place, so that those who come after us will find that a plain, easy road, which we now find rough and difficult. This difficulty is so much the greater that we are alone, and the young people are numerous; but we hope that our superiors at home, will not let us sink under the labor, particularly if God grant life to our most gracious king, whom we never cease to remember in our prayers. The country here is delightful, as it has always been described, and overflows with every blessing; so that the people live very well without being compelled to too much or too severe labor. The taxes are very light; the farmers, after their work is over, live as they do in Sweden, but are clothed as well as the respectable inhabitants of the towns. They have fresh meat and fish in abundance, and want nothing of what other countries produce; they have plenty of grain wherewith to make bread, and plenty of drink. May God continue them in the enjoyment of these blessings. There are no poor in this country, but they all provide for themselves, for the land is rich and fruitful, and no man who will labor can suffer want.

"The Indians and we are as one people; we live in much greater friendship with them than with the English: they call the Swedes in their language their own people; they were very glad when we came, as they see now that Sweden does not abandon them. They are also very fond of learning the catechism, which has been printed in their language; they like to have it read to them, and they have engaged Mr. Charles Springer to teach their children to read it. Who knows what God has yet in store for them, if our lives should be spared, when we shall have acquired their idiom? We shall spare no labor to attain that object. They go mostly naked, but many of them are clothed; they are very courteous in their behavior, and fond of obliging the Swedes; they take great pains to help them, and prevent any harm happening to them. In order to forward our designs, I hope our spiritual fathers will assist us with some of the newly printed books, particularly two church bibles, as those we have are not fit to be used in divine service; there are always opportunities between England and this country. I cannot mention, without astonishment, but to the honor of these people, that we hardly found here three Swedish books; but they were so anxious for the improvement of their children, that they lent them to one another, so that they can all read tolerably well. None of the books that his majesty graciously gave us are now out of use; they are distributed among the families, who bless the king for that valuable present, for which they are truly glad and thankful. May Almighty God preserve his majesty, the royal family, and our dear country, in peace and gladness. Though distant from it we shall never cease while we breathe, to offer up our prayers to Heaven for its prosperity."

About the same time the Rev. Mr. Rudman wrote to Professor Jacob Arrhenius, at Upsal. His statements are in agreement with those of the very interesting letter above quoted. We here give some extracts. His letter is dated 20th of October, 1697.

"Our ship arrived in Virginia, and from thence we sailed to Maryland, where we left her on the 23d of June, and proceeded up the Bay in a sloop to Elk river. There we immediately found Swedes, who heartily rejoiced at our arrival. The news of it spread through the whole country; the people came in haste from a distance of more than thirty miles, and conducted us to their places of meeting, where, after we had waited on the governor, they were called together and our credentials were read to them. Then we entered in God's name upon our holy office, I officiating to the upper congregations at Wicaco, and the Rev. Mr. Biork to the lower at Christina.

"The churches are old and in bad condition. Wherefore, with God's help we are endeavoring to build new ones. The lower one is at Christina; the upper at Wicaco, or Passyunk. The minister's garden and mansion house are at the distance of four English miles* from Philadelphia, a clever town, built by Quakers, The population is very thin and scattered, all along the river shore; so that some have sixteen miles to walk or ride to go to church. Nevertheless, they very regularly attend divine service on Sundays, etc.

"The houses are built after the Swedish

*Near Point Breeze, on the Schuylkill, where some wished the new church built, as will be seen in the sequel.

manner. The women brew excellent drink, as in Sweden; they have also a liquor made of apples or peaches, which they call cider, it is very pleasant to the taste, and very wholesome.

"In order to build our church, we are about to raise the sum of four hundred pounds sterling; but that will not be difficult, they are so very glad to have us among them; they look upon us as if we were angels from heaven. Of this they have assured me with many tears; and we may truly say, that there is no place in the world where a clergyman may be so happy and so well beloved, as in this country.

"The English have received us extremely well, and some of them even came to our meetings. We live scattered among the English and Quakers, yet our language is preserved as pure as any where in Sweden. There are about twelve hundred persons that speak it. There are also Welshmen, who speak their own mother tongue, besides Englishmen, Dutchmen, and some Frenchmen. Almost every one can read, at which we are much rejoiced. God be thanked for his goodness, which has never yet been wanting to us.

"As to the government, it is very mild, and the people live quietly under Governor William Markham, who is exceedingly well-disposed towards us. He has reproached us with not going often enough to see him, and has left us quite at liberty as to our church discipline. There are many Swedes employed in the administration of this government; some of them are counsellors, whom they call judges; many of them are officers, captains, constables, ensigns, etc. There is plenty of work for us. We are alone; our congregations are scattered, our youth numerous, and but few that do not require instruction. We have schools and churches to build, etc. etc."

CHAPTER V.

It was an important matter to have good churches, in which the different congregations might attend for divine worship, as those that were found here were decayed, and scarcely habitable. The first thing, therefore, that occupied the attention of these worthy missionaries was the erection, at once, of two commodious edifices in which to hold divine service; one for the lower congregation, and one for the upper. How the Swedes at Christina proceeded with the work there, will appear from the following extracts of a letter written by the Rev. Mr. Biork to the Hon. Charles Wystrom, dated 19th of November, 1700.

"Shortly after my arrival at this place, I persuaded the congregation to agree in selecting a better place for a church than Tranhook, to wit, Christina; and I immediately commenced the work in the Lord's name, though with little money: but I never doubted, notwithstanding my unworthiness, of divine assistance. I therefore made a bargain with bricklayers and carpenters, and bound them and me so strongly, that otherwise the work would not have been finished in less than three years. We laid the first stone at the north corner on the 28th of May, 1698. The size of the church,* inside of the walls, is sixty feet in length, thirty feet in breadth, and twenty feet in height. The walls are of hard gray stone up to the windows, and three and a half feet thick; but above that only two feet.

"There are four doors; a large one at the west end, and a similar one at the south: there are two smaller ones on the north side, one of which leads into the vestry-room. There are two windows on the north, and two on the south, all of the same size; but there is a larger one at the east end, and a small one over the western door. There is a small belfry at the east end. The roof is arched with logs, and plastered. It is covered with cedar shingles.

"The pews in the church are made of fir; the chancel is circular, and the inner banister, as well as the pulpit, of walnut wood, well turned. There is a large aisle, eight feet in breadth, from the chancel to the large door, and across the aisle from the north door to that on the south. Between the chancel and the first row of pews there is also a little way with six pews on each side, to the cross aisle. There are also long pews along the wall for the men, from the south door to the east end; and there

*This church is still standing and occasionally occupied for divine service. (1858.)

are seats in the chancel for the ministers. In the lower part of the church, from the north and south doors to that on the west, there is a large aisle, with eight pews on each side."

The church thus erected, with a zeal and enterprise so praiseworthy, was, on Trinity Sunday, in the following year, 1699, dedicated to the service of Almighty God. On that occasion, the Rev. Mr. Rudman preached the sermon, having taken his text from Psalm cxxvi. 3:— "The Lord hath done great things for us, whereof we are glad." The name of Trinity church was given to the building, in honor of the Triune God. "Mr. Rudman and I," says Mr. Biork, "were clad in white surplices, made after our manner, as well as could be done; but other church vestments could not be procured here. The Rev. Mr. Auren preached afterwards at the celebration of the Lord's Supper, where we made a collection of about two hundred dollars; for there were many hundred persons present, of all religions, whom I entertained afterwards with meat and drink in the best manner I could. The neighbors all around partook of the feast, and several carried provisions home with them."

Over the large window, at the east end of the church, iron letters were built in the wall, with the following abbreviated Latin sentence:

Lux L. I. tenebr. oriens ex alto.*

* Light springing from Heaven shineth in darkness.

Over the large door, at the west end, in the same kind of letters, is the following:

1698

Si De. pro nobis Quis contra nos.*
†Sub Imp. Reg. D. G. Ang.
WILL. III.
Propr. Will. Penn, Vice Gub. Will.
Magnif. Reg. Suec. Nunc Glor. Memor.
CAROL. XI.
Huc ableg:
E T B.
W S.
P L.

Over the door on the south side, was the word,

IMMANUEL

And on the north side, the following sentence:

Pol. NR. CHRIST.‡

The Swedes near Philadelphia commenced their preparations for the building of a new church, at the same time with those of Chris-

* If God be for us, who can be agains us.

† Under the reign of William III, by the grace of God King of England, William Penn, being Proprietary, and William, [Markham] Vice Governor; Charles XI. one of the illustrious kings of Sweden, now of glorious memory sent to this place E. T. Biork, etc.

‡ Christ, our king, has rule.

tina; but the undertaking was delayed for a year or two, on account of their not being able to agree among themselves as to where the building should be erected. Those who resided on the banks of the Schuylkill, and lower down, wished the church to be built at a place called Passyunk, (now Point Breeze,) where the clergyman resided on a glebe belonging to the congregation. On the other hand, the Swedes near to Philadelphia, and higher up, wished it built at Wicaco, on the Delaware, half a mile below the city, though now within its limits. It was here the old church stood. It was now considered not worth repairing. There was also a burial ground here, in which the Swedish families, on both sides of the river, had for many years interred their dead. Neither Wicaco, nor Passyunk was entirely central in its location; and wherever the church might have been built, a large part of the congregation would have still had to travel several miles in getting to it.

As far as Mr. Rudman himself, expressed an opinion on this question, he preferred having the church at Passyunk, as being more convenient to his residence. But he was not tenacious on this point, and was only anxious for harmony and peace. Many conferences having resulted in no decision of the question, a general meeting of the congregation was finally called on the 17th of May, 1698. A tedious discussion of the subject proving fruitless, the lower inhabitants proposed to have the matter decided by lot. To this the upper members were at first opposed, but through the persuasions of Mr. Rudman were induced afterwards to agree. Having by prayer and singing invoked the blessing of God on the undertaking, two pieces of paper were prepared, on one of which was written *Wicaco,* and on the other *Passyunk;* these were shaken in a hat, and thrown upon the ground, when, upon taking one up, and opening it, the name of *Wicaco* appeared. Dissension at once ceased, and all joined in a cheerful hymn of praise. At the same time the agreement was ratified by the following persons signing their names to a suitable instrument of writing, viz: Andrew Rudman, Capt. Lorence Cox, Andrew Bancson, Caspar Fish, Peter Rambo, Gustavus Justis, Elias Toy, Michael Lycon, Charles Springer, Andrew Rambo, Matthias Morton, Gabriel Cox, John Cox, jr. Hans Boon, Nich. Lycon, Richard Rhodes, Gunnar Swanson, Christian Clæson, Laurence Holstein.

Jonas Biurstroem, witness.

After the above settlement of the dispute in relation to the site for the church, there was difficulty and uneasiness in another form. The family of Swan Swanson (then spelled Svan Svanson) had given the ground on which the old church stood,* and had lately increased it part of an acre; but the congregation desired a small addition down to the river, in order to prevent ship-building in front of the church, and the danger which would thereby be incurred from fire; they also wished for permission to build a small house for the sexton, to guard the church from injury. With some difficulty the first request was granted, the other denied. This denial led to fresh dissatisfaction; in con-

* As the question is often asked, by what tenure does the Wicaco church hold its property, it is thought proper to give the following information. That on which the church stands, containing one acre and a half and five perches, was given, as above remarked, by the Swanson family. The deed is from Catharine Swanson, widow of Swan Swanson; Swan Boon, and Brigita, his wife, one of the daughters of Swan Swanson; Hans Boon, and Barbara, his wife, another of the daughters; and Peter Bankson, and Catharine, his wife, a third daughter.

Also, an acre of ground, north of the church, on which the old parsonage stood, and the present one (built in 1832) now stands, was given by Hans Boon, and Barbara, his wife, "for the use, benefit and behoof of the minister of the Swedish congregation for the time being, and his successors forever."

There is a third deed, dated 19th June, 1719, from Martha Cock, daughter of John Cock and Margaret, his wife, one of the daughters of Swan Swanson, to Peter Rambo, John Stille, John Scute, and Jesta Jestason, for twenty-five acres of land, lying near the Wicaco church, in trust, "for the use, benefit and behoof of the minister of the Swedish congregation for the time being, and his successors forever, in the nature of glebe land, etc." These twenty-five acres were purchased by the congregation for *ninety pounds.*

sequence of which Mr. Rudman, in order to accommodate both the upper and lower members of the parish, proposed that the new church should be built at Passyunk, and the old one at Wicaco be repaired, and that divine service should be held part of the year in one, and part in the other. This proposal was not acceded to. Mr. R. wearied with this unpleasant state of things, had for some time been threatening to leave them. Accordingly, on the seventh Sunday after Trinity, being the 31st of July, 1698, he concluded his sermon with a feeling address, in which he reminded them of his unceasing parochial labors, and his repeated efforts to unite them, but that having failed in the object of his wishes, he had come to the determination to leave them, and would take that opportunity of bidding them farewell. He soon after went to Christina, where he remained until the sixth of September.

After the departure of Mr. Rudman, Mr. Biork visited the congregation, and preached for them on the tenth Sunday after Trinity, the Gospel for which day relates the weeping of Christ over Jerusalem. His exertions had a good effect. The congregation were brought to a better mind, and sent deputies to Christina, desiring a conference with the Rev. Messrs. Rudman and Biork. These deputies were instructed to ask forgiveness, to submit the whole matter in dispute to the decision of these clergymen, to renew their subscriptions for the church, and to secure future harmony by fining any person ten pounds who should again cause any dispute. We would not omit to remark, that the Rev. Mr. Auren also had aided in restoring the people to a state of harmony and peace.

Mr. Rudman, equally anxious with the congregation to see differences healed, went back with the deputies, resolved to meet future difficulties with christian forbearance—"sensible," to use his own language, "that the ministers of God have little else to expect but trouble." He took advantage, without delay, of the present favorable circumstances; procured a written assurance of the ground to the river; obtained the governor's consent to what was proposed to be done, and for a bridge or ferry across the Schuylkill, for the convenience of the people on the other side; and made arrangements to bring materials for the new church at Wicaco, from the old one at Tinicum. All of which, on the thirteenth Sunday after Trinity, was in proper form proclaimed in the English language.

The same bricklayers and carpenters who had built the church at Christina, were employed to build the one at Wicaco; and the work went on so successfully, that on the second day of July, being the first Sunday after Trinity, in the year 1700, every thing was finished; and on that day the dedication took place, when the Rev. Mr. Biork preached from 2 Sam. v. 29: "Therefore, now let it please thee to bless the house of thy servant, that it may continue forever before thee: for thou, O Lord God, hast spoken it; and with thy blessing let the house of thy servant be blessed forever." On this occasion there were a great many English persons and others present from Philadelphia,* for whose benefit Mr. Biork delivered a summary of his discourse in the English language.

"This church," says Mr. Biork, in one of his letters to Sweden, "is of the same size as the other, only that one of the corners is shortened in order to make room for a belfry or steeple, which has been begun at the west end, but must remain some time unfinished, in order to see whether God will bless us so far as that we may have a bell, and in what manner we can procure it. This church is built of stone to the top of the foundation, but not so good as that of which the lower church is built. The buildings will cost us, according to our reckoning, about twenty thousand dollars, Swedish money, and something more; of which I am yet indebted in five thousand dollars, and my colleague is in about the same situation. We have nothing to rely on but the efforts of the congregations to raise that money as well as they can.

* The church, now within the limits of the city, was then some distance from it.

"Thus, through God's blessing, we have completed the great work, and built two fine churches, superior to any built in this country, particularly that at Christina; so that the English themselves, who now govern this province, and are beyond measure richer than we are, wonder at what we have done. It is but lately that two governors, with their suites, have come to this place, and visited our churches. The one is Francis Nicholson, governor of Maryland, and our great patron; the other is named Blackstone, and is governor of Virginia. With all this we want some ornaments for our church, which are not to be procured here, such as a couple of bells, handsome chalices and pattens, and chandeliers or lustres. We have also room for a small organ. If we should obtain these things through the generosity of those who are able and willing to honor themselves by honoring their Maker, we shall consider it as a particular mark of divine favor, and their names shall be recorded as benefactors of our church. In the meanwhile, we are well satisfied with the blessings that we have received from Almighty God; we hope he will preserve our country from the war* that is impending, and seems to threaten Sweden. We hope also that in time we shall have obtained the things that we most want, particularly books. I have at

*The succession war for the crown of Spain, in which England was engaged against France.

last established a school here, with an able teacher at the head of it, who also serves as parish clerk, an office which I was before obliged to perform. Things are not yet on such a steady footing as I could wish, but I shall do all I can, and no man can do more.

"Our congregations more and more require our care and attention. My colleague and I do all in our power to have divine service performed here as in Sweden; we instruct the people in their catechism; we travel from place to place, and from house to house; in short, we do all in our power to fulfil the important duties that are imposed upon us."

The two churches being thus completed, it was the next wish of the rectors, as the foregoing letter shows, to obtain the things of which they stood most in need. The letter speaks of a "a couple of bells, handsome chalices, pattens, and chandeliers or lustres." Nothing is said about a *Baptismal Font,* for each church; yet no people laid more stress, than the Swedes, on the importance of having their children early dedicated to the Lord in the holy sacrament of Baptism. As, therefore, the above letter is silent on the subject of a Baptismal Font for each church, while the less important articles of *bells* and *chandeliers* are mentioned, we may infer that this necessary article had been provided, and been long in use in their earlier churches. In the Wicaco Church there is now a large baptismal font, of marble, unlike those belonging to the Episcopal churches in this country, but such as is common in Sweden. This font has been in the church from time immemorial. The probability is, it was brought or sent over from the mother country at a very early period.

I may here mention that there is still preserved in this church, on the front of the west gallery, an antique representation of two cherubs, with their wings spread over what is intended to represent the Holy Bible; on one of the open pages of which is the following passage from Isaiah, in Swedish characters:—"The people who walked in darkness have seen a great light," etc.; and on the other page that passage (also in Swedish characters) from the New Testament, in which the angels, at the birth of the Saviour, are spoken of as celebrating the event in the anthem of—"Glory to God in the Highest," etc.

The present Bell of the Wicaco church has the following inscription upon it:

"Cast for Swedish Church in Philadelphia, styled Gloria Dei, partly from the old bell dated 1643.

G. HEDDERLY, FECIT, 1806.

I to the Church the living call,
And to the grave do summon all."

CHAPTER VI.

The king of Sweden having promised the Rev. Mr. Rudman and his colleague leave to return home after a few years, he, in the year 1701, with the advice of the archbishop, Dr. Benzelius, appointed the Rev. Andrew Sandel to come over, and take charge of the Wicaco church. This gentleman left Sweden on the 21st of August of that year; and after some detention in England, and the usual tedious passage of those days across the Atlantic, arrived in the Delaware on the 12th of March, following, and had his first interview with Mr. Rudman on the 18th of the same month. Mr. Rudman's intention now was to return to Sweden; but the Dutch inhabitants of New York and Albany having been for many years without a preacher, invited him to settle among them. Their destitute condition, and the fear lest they might fall away from the pure faith of the Gospel, induced him to comply with their request. He accordingly preached his farewell sermon at Wicaco on the 19th of July, and departed the next day to enter upon the duties of his new charge.

How long Mr. Rudman officiated in New York is not known. He found, however, that the climate did not agree with his constitution, and his health becoming impaired, he took measures to procure for them a Dutch clergyman to supply his place. A student of divinity, by the name of Justus Falkner, arrived, who was ordained in Wicaco church by the Rev. Messrs. Rudman, Biork, and Sandel.* After leaving New York, Mr. Rudman officiated for some time at the English church at Oxford; and afterwards, upon the Rev. Mr. Evans leaving this for England, he took charge of Christ Church in this city. He continued to officiate in that until his death, which took place on the 17th of September, 1708, aged forty years. His remains lie beneath the chancel in the Wicaco Church. He appears to have been much beloved by the Swedes of that period, and their descendants will long hold in grateful remembrance his self-denial and faithfulness as a minister of Christ. The stone over his grave has the following inscription:

* This ordination by presbyters, instead of by a bishop, was the best their situation, or the circumstances in which they were placed, enabled them to obtain. A sister church wanted a pastor, and they had to decide between letting them go unsupplied, or giving them one with defective orders. When persons were to be ordained under circumstances that prevented the presence of a Bishop, it was usual for the Archbishop of Upsal to issue his mandamus to certain presbyters to act in his stead.

This monument covers the remains of the Rev. ANDREW RUDMAN. Being sent hither from Sweden, he first founded and built this church—was a constant and faithful preacher in the English, Swedish and Dutch churches, eleven years in this country, where he advanced true piety by sound doctrine and good example. He died September 17, A. D. 1708, aged 40 years.

The year after Mr. Sandel had taken charge of the congregation, a meeting was called to take into consideration the state of the church walls, which had perceptibly given way. A large majority of the persons present were in favor of strengthening them by means of iron work; but before coming to any final conclusion, it was deemed advisable to consult on the subject, some person of approved judgment. A committee, consisting of Matthias Keen, Hans Lycon, John Cox, and Peter Bankson, was appointed to consult with a Mr. Peter Deal, who was thought a competent judge. This committee reported that Mr. Deal was of opinion that porches built on each side of the church, would be the best means of strengthening the walls. This plan, though more expensive than the other, of iron clamps, was unanimously approved, especially as one wing would answer for a vestry-room, and the other for a vestibule or entrance to the church. A subscription was at once opened for the purpose and the persons present put down their names for £109 4*s*. Mr. Sandel complains that this building gave him a great deal of trouble—many of the subscribers being backward in making payment, though the wardens were attentive to their duties. The workmen were anxious to be paid, and he was obliged, with one of the wardens, to go from house to house to collect what was due.

On the 3d of February, 1704, John Evans, a Welshman, arrived from England as governor of the province; on which occasion the Rev. Mr. Sandel, and fifteen of the oldest members of the congregation, paid their respects to him.

In 1705 the upper inhabitants* made application for occasional services in their neighborhood in the winter season, because of their distance from the church. It was agreed that the rector should officiate there twice during the winter season.

Very soon after the church was built, arrangements were made for renting the pews. It is proper to mention this, because in our time there are a few persons, descendants of the ancient Swedes, who claim all the rights appertaining to membership, such as the right to bury in the Swedish ground, the right to vote at elections, etc. simply because their forefathers assisted in building the church, or purchasing the ground, and independently of any present payment of pew rent. This claim is unreasonable and contrary to ancient usage.

* Meaning, I suppose, those at Upper Merion, or perhaps, up the Delaware towards Bristol.

It was never intended by those who built the church, or purchased the lands belonging to the church, that their posterity should enjoy such rights absolutely, and without any restriction. At a meeting of the congregation, held on the first of May, A. D. 1705, the following resolution was adopted:—"Those who, with their families, remove from our congregation, and cannot, or will not attend divine worship, or will not submit to the rules of the church, shall themselves and heirs lose their rights altogether." If rights, then, could be lost within five years of the time when the church was built, and by those who had helped to build it, why should their posterity, at this late period, hold such rights by a tenure admitting of no restriction?

About this time (1705) another donation of books was received from Sweden, consisting of bibles, prayer books, primers, and spiritual meditations. They were a present from the reigning sovereign, Charles XII. They were equally divided between the church at Wicaco and that at Christina.

As my plan is to mention facts as they occurred, or in chronological order. it is proper here to lay before the reader an address of the Swedes, to the Legislature of the Province, setting forth certain grievances which the document itself sufficiently explains.

"To the Representatives of the Province of Pennsylvania, met in General Assembly at Philadelphia, this first day of June, 1709. The complaint of divers of the freeholders and others settlers of this Province;

Setteth forth:

"That whereas we, the Swedes, ancient settlers and first inhabitants of this Province, with great difficulty, hazard and loss of several of our lives, have at last obtained peace and quietness with the Indians—and after the changes that have happened by reason of the divers sorts of governments, we have lived peaceably and quietly, enjoying our lands and estates, which we first settled, under our own government. And since we are informed that upon the surrendering of this province to the crown of England, in lieu of Surinam to the Dutch, it was agreed on both sides, that the inhabitants were in no wise to be disturbed either in their lives, liberties, or estates; we after that, being summoned to appear before the government, which then resided in New York, were obliged to take patents or grants for what land we held before, or desired after. But since this Province has been granted to William Penn, he and his officers called for our patents and grants under pretence of renewing them, which having obtained, would not return them again, but instead thereof re-surveyed great parts of our lands, and took it from some of us; others were required to pay greater quitrents than before; and because some of us refused the payment of such quitrents, being on some tracts of land three or four times more than we ought, or used to pay, when under the government of New York; we being, as we suppose, the Queen's tenants, and not liable to pay any at all to the proprietor—the collector, James Logan, threatened to make distress upon our goods for the said rents, using at the same time many harsh and opprobrious epithets.

"We, therefore, presuming that the same justice which, under similar cases, is dispensed by the Parliament of England, may be obtained here, solicit from you our representatives, some help in our distress, that we may have our patents restored to us, together with all the overplus of the quitrents which have been unjustly exacted from us these twenty years past. For which we shall always pray:*

Zacharias Cock,
Eric Keen,
John Tanck,
Otto Earnest Cock,
Peter Peterson,
John Aretson,
Matthias Nezelius,
Anders Bonde,
Anders Mortenson,
Valentine Kock,
Andrew Longacre,
John Mortenson,
Gabriel Cock,
John Stille,
Hans George,
Morten Mortenson,
Gosta Gostason,
Hans Bonde,
Lors Mortenson,
Olle Bonde,
Gabriel Friend,
John Ellet,
John Hindrickson,
Matthias Keen."

* What was the result of the above application to the Legislature, I have seen nothing to show. The grievance complained of seems to have been such as required redress.

At a meeting of the congregation on the 18th of May, A. D. 1710, the usual election for vestrymen took place. It may be of use to the Swedes of our time to know what were then considered to be the duties of vestrymen. These duties were declared to be—"1st. To take care of the church, see to its repairs, and, if necessary, put up additional buildings. 2d. To maintain the parochial ordinances and regulations enacted at the general meetings, and to preserve order in time of divine worship. 3d. To inspect the behavior of the people in their respective districts, admonish those that misbehave, and proceed with them further, if necessary. 4th. To attend divine worship often, partake of the Lord's Supper, and be edifying examples in all Christian virtues."

At the same meeting the following resolution was adopted:—"Whereas some, when reproved for their sins, and are not permitted to break our church rules, hate both the minister and the congregation, and abandon divine worship; therefore resolved that such shall be several times admonished, and warned against the dreadful hazard of their souls; and if they persevere in their malice, shall have no right to the privileges of the church; and if they die without repentance, shall not be buried in our cemetery."

In the month of May, A. D. 1712, two clergymen, Andrew Hesselius, master of Philosophy, and Mr. Abraham Lidenius, arrived from Sweden, sent by the Government and Bishop Swedburg, to take charge of the church at Christina, in place of the Rev. Mr. Biork, who had been recalled to Sweden. His recall was by Charles XII. in the following words:

"Charles, by the grace of God king of Sweden, etc., etc. To all whom it may concern, greeting: His royal majesty, our beloved father, of glorious memory, had a tender solicitude for the welfare of those Swedish children that removed to the far distant country of America, and particularly for their constancy in the true evangelical doctrines, and the pure worship of God. We have likewise the same pious and laudable zeal. Having recalled the Rev. Eric Biork, who in the year 1697, was by his aforesaid Royal Majesty sent to a Swedish congregation in that country, to be rewarded for his long and laborious services, by some comfortable situation in our kingdom; and being desirous to provide this our congregation with a spiritual guardian in his place, we have appointed a man renowned for his learning, official talents, piety, and grave manners, our faithful subject, the Rev. Andrew Hagvinius. We have also commissioned the Rev. ——— as a colleague, for aid in preaching and other clerical functions; and sent a donation of bibles, and many books of common prayer, to be distributed among the congregations. They will, no doubt, be pleased and edified by the services of these clergymen. These may also depend on a gracious promotion in Sweden, when they shall wish to return. We also assure the congregations and the Swedes living in the aforesaid country, of our particular and permanent royal favor; commending them to the care of Almighty God.

"Written in our Head Quarters at Smorgonie, in Littaven, February 21, A. D. 1708.

CHARLES."

Mr. Hagvinius, the clergyman mentioned in the preceding document, died while preparing for the voyage; in consequence of which the Rev. Mr. Hesselius, above referred to, was commissioned to take the place of the Rev. Mr. Biork, with the other gentleman here spoken of, as his assistant.

Doctor Jesper Swedburg, Bishop of Scara, in the province of West Gothia, had been appointed superintendent of the Swedish Mission, and recommended the aforesaid clergymen. The following is an extract from the letter which he sent by them to the congregation:— "You receive now, my beloved brethren and sisters in Christ, two pious and learned clergymen, with a stock of religious books. This fresh proof of God's merciful goodness, and the king's solicitude for your spiritual welfare, merits your sincere gratitude, which you will display in a truly christian life, and thereby insure the same blessings in future. I am confident that these clergymen will faithfully perform their duties, and shall be very happy to hear that you have received them with hearty affection. Having promoted their appointment by a zealous recommendation, I shall always, while God preserves my life, with the greatest satisfaction employ all the means in my power for your benefit. May God have you all in his holy keeping; abundantly bless you and your children, and finally grant us a meeting in heaven with everlasting felicity."

The wish expressed in the foregoing letter, that the congregation here would receive the clergymen sent them "with hearty affection," was not in this, or in any other instance disappointed. It was a beautiful feature in the character of the Swedes that they felt a deep interest in the great concerns of religion, and set a high value on the means of grace imparted through the ministry of the Church. They well knew how to appreciate the sentiment expressed by St. Paul, where he asks, "How shall they call on him in whom they have not believed? And how shall they believe in him of whom they have not heard? And how shall they hear without a preacher?" They loved their ministers as "ambassadors of Christ," commissioned and appointed to "beseech them, in Christ's stead to be reconciled to God." And this seems to have been *universal* among them, or nearly so. Long distances (ten or fifteen miles) were often walked, that they might join in the prayers and praises of the Church, and hear from the lips of their ministers the precious truths of the Gospel. But they had been well trained up. Faithfulness in the clergy will usually produce piety in the people. The Swedish missionaries were generally laborious and faithful in the performance of their duties. And that seems to be the general character of the clergy in Sweden. J. Macdonald, in his travels through Denmark and Sweden, in 1809, (vol. 2, page 105) thus speaks of them: "The clergy of this kingdom are a valuable and virtuous order, and are usually allowed to be as active and benevolent as in the best governed States in Europe." The same writer says of the *laity*, that a *gentleman* there is never seen intoxicated.

Old Swedes' Church
SCATTERGOOD

CHAPTER VII.

For a considerable time after the new church at Wicaco was built, the residence of the clergyman continued to be at Passyunk, four miles below the church, on the Schuylkill. Among the church records I find the following memorandum, in the hand-writing of the late Dr. Collin. It purports to be "a translation from the Wicaco church records." The memorandum is as follows: The parsonage on Passyunk was bought by, or from Andrew Bengtson, containing eighty acres of land, whereof seventy are situated near the minister's house, and ten on Ponskon-hook. It cost in all sixty pounds. Was slso bought by or from Captain Laurence Cock, sixteen acres, of which the cost was ten pounds. Afterwards was purchased on Wicaco, as the church was built there, as a glebe, the share of Valentine Cock, under a proper title, as appears from the deed of purchase dated the 19th of September, 1698. The cost of this was twenty-five pounds. The land was paid for in the following manner: First was sold the parsonage on Tinicum for one hundred pounds, agreeably to the consent of both congregations. Of this the Christina congregation received fifty pounds, and Wicaco the same amount. As this money was not sufficient, the people resolved to contribute five shillings each family, and to make a present of the surplus to the church. N. B. This was done in Mr. Rudman's time. Mr. Sandel and the congregation bought in 1719, from Martha Swanson,* twenty-five acres on Wicaco. Gunnar Swanson, who died in 1702, left to the church one-third of his estate."

This is a memorandum of some importance, and gives us a view of all the property, I suppose, ever owned by the church. I have never seen the deed here said to be of the date of 19th of September, 1698, and was before ignorant † that so much land had been purchased at that early period. A question here suggests itself: *What has become of all this land?* And the proper answer would seem to be—that a great deal of it has fallen into other hands, *through neglect*. One of our late wardens,‡ recently informed me that property which now yields an income of several hundred dollars to the church was a few years since not known to belong to it, and was quite accidentally recovered

*The deed says Martha Cock, granddaughter of Swan Swanson.

†Further inquiry induces the belief that this purchase of 1698 was never made. It appears that before 1719, the church owned no property at Wicaco, except two or three acres, on part of which the church is built.

‡Mr. William Jones.

by him out of the hands of a person who, about forty or fifty years ago had rented it as a grass lot, and afterwards *brought himself to believe that he was the owner.**

The parsonage house in Passyunk was accidentally burnt down in 1717, and was immediately rebuilt. We have in the old records a very particular account of who furnished the timber, who cut it; who hauled it; who built the walls; who cut the rafters; who carried them to the ground; who put them up; who bought the shingles; who shaved them, etc. The reader *who is curious in such matters*, may see all the particulars on application to the rector of the church.

The 11th of November, 1717, is the date of an instrument of writing, by which Charles XII. of Sweden, recalled the Rev. Mr. Sandel from his duties here, and appointed him rector of Hedemora, a town in Dalecarlia. The recall was received on the 28th of May, 1718; but private and parochial concerns prevented his immediate departure. The latter had reference, chiefly, to the purchase of the twenty-five acres of land which about this time the church was contracting for with Martha Cock, a grand-daughter, as already mentioned, of Swan Swan-

* Of the ninety-six acres once owned by the church, on the Schuylkill, and mentioned in the above memoradum, a considerable portion has been lost *through posscssion of more than twenty-one years!*

son, deceased. His last meeting with the congregation was on the 7th of May, 1719; on which occasion the Rev. Mr. Hesselius, of Christina church, and the Rev. Mr. Lidenius pastor of Racoon church, in Jersey, were present. These clergymen promised to perform divine service once a month, during the vacancy. And Arvid Hernbom, a student of good abilities, and who for some years kept school in the parish, agreed with them and the people to keep the church open on the other Sundays by acting as lay-reader.

We have no data from which to ascertain with much precision what was the order of divine service among the Swedes, in the times of which we are writing. Mr. Sandel has mentioned that, "the forenoon service was observed in the manner required by our (the Swedish) liturgy, and as is customary in Sweden." He also says that they had two sermons on Sunday: that they used the "Te Deum," to which I suppose he refers, when he says they sang "O Lord we praise thee." As to the preaching, it seems to have been frequently from a portion of the catechism. Mr. S. was in the habit, in the summer season, of walking through the aisles, and examining the congregation on the catechism, and on their knowledge of the sermon he had previously preached. Such a practice in our time would be apt to make thin churches.

Mr. Sandal speaks of the harmony and friendship that existed between the Swedish and English congregations, and that they had mutually officiated in each other's churches.* "On solemn occasions," he says, "as at the laying of the corner stones of churches, they have always invited us, and conducted themselves as

* The Swedish clergymen did not not confine themselves, in their endeavors to be useful, to the particular churches of which they had the pastoral charge. The Rev. Mr. Hesselius, pastor of the church at Christina, seems particularly to have labored in a wider sphere than his own congregation. That excellent institution, "The Society for the Propagation of the Gospel in Foreign Parts," to which the Episcopal church in this country owes such a large debt of gratitude, noticed and rewarded the labors of Mr. Hesselius, as appears from the following letter to him of its Secretary:

London, May 8th, 1721.

Reverend Sir:

The Society for the Propagation of the Gospel in Foreign Parts, hath received a representation from the clergy in Pennsylvania, setting forth, among other things, the good services you have done by reading prayers and preaching in the several vacant churches in Pennsylvania, and have ordered me to acquaint you, that in consideration of your past labors, they have presented you with the sum of ten pounds, for which you may draw on their treasurer. They have also agreed to allow you ten pounds per annum, in case you perform divine service and preach in the English language in the several vacant churches in Pennsylvania, at least twenty times in one year, and transmit over hither proper certificates thereof.

I am, Reverend Sir,

Your most humble servant,

DAVID HUMPHREYS, *Sec'y.*

friends to our church. This year they undertook to enlarge their church, and though the Presbyterians offered them the use of their church, they asked to be permitted to worship in Wicaco, which was granted them for three successive Sundays. And for confirming the unity that existed between the two congregations, a Swedish hymn was sung at the English service. To preserve unity and confidence with the English church, the present Bishop Dr. Swedburg, has continually urged in his letters."

The Swedes, about this time, addressed a long letter to "the Right Honorable Count Jyttenborg, the Swedish Envoy in London," on the subject of the grievances which had led them in 1709, to lay their complaint before the Legislature of the Province of Pennsylvania. This letter appears to have been designed merely as a vindication of themselves against what they conceived to be "misrepresentations of William Penn, and his commissioners." An extract will show the nature of the misunderstanding between them and Mr. Penn:

May it please your Excellency,

"We are much concerned that Mr. Penn should complain of us in such general terms as renders it difficult to make any particular defence, as he seems to do in our case. We can with all sincerity assure your Excellency, that we and our predecessors, have been ready upon all occasions to serve Mr. Penn, and never, as far as we know, gave him the least cause of complaint. But the manifest wrongs we received, gave us frequent and just occasion to complain. That this may appear, we respectfully ask your impartial consideration of our case and grievances, which in part may appear to your Excellency in these following particulars, viz:

"When this country was surrendered to the English, all the inhabitants were confirmed in their lands, but required by the Governor of New York (to whom they were then annexed) to take patents out there for the same, and to become tenants to the kings of England, under the rent of a bushel of wheat per annum, for every hundred acres. But, may it please your Excellency, when this province was granted to the present governor by the late King Charles II. we find, that lands held by the Indians, and not the lands confirmed before to our predecessors, much less the rents reserved to the crown of England, were granted to Mr. Penn; who, nevertheless, by an order under his hand and provincial seal, dated the 14th of June, 1683, did require all that had no patents, or were willing to have their patents renewed, to send their certificates of survey and old patents, to the surveyor general's office; whereupon many of the said patents and certificates were taken in, and have been detained ever since from the owners; and instead of having patents upon the said certificates of survey, or the old patents renewed, the governor and his commissioners caused the lands therein mentioned, without any warrant of law, or consent of the possessors, to be actually surveyed, and the greatest and best part thereof patented to new purchasers under Mr. Penn; and the rents of what was left, advanced on some three, on others fourfold, more than was reserved by the old patents," etc.

We give the above complaint as we find it, without comment. We are not sufficiently versed in ancient law to know what were the respective rights of Mr. Penn, as proprietor of Pennsylvania, and of the Swedes as earlier possessors of part of the soil. *Non nostrum tantas componere lites.* It appears to us, however, that they had some ground for complaint.

The Rev. Mr. Sandel, has noted some meteorological, and other occurrences which happened in his time. He states that on Michaelmas-day, the 10th of October, 1703, a quantity of snow fell, that laid on the ground for twenty-four hours; and that the oldest people said such a thing had not happened before in their time. On the 18th of the same month, in the evening, a hurricane arose, which did great damage. In Maryland and Virginia, many vessels were cast away, several driven to sea, and no more heard of. Roofs of houses were torn off, and large trees blown down. The same storm reached to England, where also it was destructive.

In 1704, in the latter part of November and December, and in January, 1705, there were many great and lasting snow-storms. Few persons could remember so severe a winter.

The winter of 1708, was very cold; and it continued so, very late. On the 5th of April, the cold was so intense, that water thrown on the ground at noon, immediately froze.

For six weeks, in June, July, and August, 1705, there was a great deal of bad weather.

The beginning of 1714, was uncommonly warm. Mr. S. saw a wild flower in the woods on the 8th of Feburary. The Spring was also very mild. Some rye was in ear on the 10th of April.

There was an appearance of locusts in 1715, of which Mr. Sandel has given the following account: "In May, 1715, a multitude of locusts came out of the ground every where, even on the solid roads. They were wholly covered with a shell, and it seemed very wonderful that they could with this penetrate the hard earth. Having come out of the earth, they crept out of the shells, flew away, sat down on the trees, and made a peculiar noise until evening. Being spread over the country in such numbers, the noise they made was so loud that the cow-bells could scarcely be heard in the woods. They pierced the bark on the branches of trees, and deposited their eggs in the opening. Many apprehended that the trees would wither in consequence of this, but no symptom of it was observed next year. Hogs and poultry fed on them. Even the Indians did eat them, especially when they first came, boiling them a little. This made it probable that they were of the same kind as those eaten by John the Baptist. They did not continue long, but died in the month of June.

The same year was very fruitful. A bushel of wheat cost two shillings, or two shillings and three-pence; a bushel of corn, twenty-two pence; of rye, twenty pence. A barrel of cider cost six shillings.

It is elsewhere remarked, that in the latter part of November, 1732, "ice made the river impassable;" and that in January 1733, there was much snow.

Mr. Sandel is not the only one who has related the following "stratagem" of Governor Evans. In 1706, May 27th, he caused a false report to circulate, that the French were coming up to Philadelphia, with a view to take the town by storm, and that they were already high up the river. This report produced great fear and consternation. Having collected his soldiers, he caused ramparts to be erected on Society-hill,* where he placed field pieces. He

*Mr. Watson, in his ANNALS OF PHILADELPHIA, speaks of Society-hill as a place much resorted to, in former times,

ordered the soldiers to keep themselves in readiness, as the enemy would be up with the next tide. The people were very much alarmed. The Quakers conveyed their wives and children into the woods; their moveables they either carried off, or hid in wells. Those that lived near the town carried their goods into the swamp, and also hid themselves there. Many women in a delicate situation, miscarried, in consequence of their fright. This false alarm was raised to see what course the Quakers would take, and whether they would fight. Such conduct in a governor, needs no comment.

Another circumstance, not connected with our Swedish story is the following: In 1715 the Indians living on the border of the Mississippi, made an incursion into the western parts of South Carolina, and destroyed a great many of the white inhabitants. As soon as the alarm

on account of a spring there, called "Bathsheba's Spring." I have in my possession a manuscript life of my great-grandmother, Ann Clay, in which she speaks of this spring in the following terms:—"Under Society-hill, she (her maiden aunt) built a small house close by the best spring of water, perhaps, that was in our city. This house she furnished with books, a table, and a cup, in which she, or any that visited her, drank of the spring. What name she gave her new house I know not; but some people gave it the name of Bathsheba's Bower, (her name was Bathsheba Bowers.) As for the spring, it has ever since borne the name of 'Bathsheba's Spring.'"

was given, the people of the adjacent country fled from their homes to Charleston; but as that town could not contain them all, many took passage in the trading vessels, and went, some to Barbadoes, and others to New England and Philadelphia. The massacre was occasioned by the bad faith observed towards the Indians by the traders living among them.

CHAPTER VIII.

The next pastor appointed for the church Gloria Dei, (Wicaco,) was the Rev. Jonas Lidman. His appointment was in the following terms, viz.

"We, Ulrica Eleanora, by the grace of God Queen of the Swedes, etc. etc. make known, that as by the promotion of the Rev. Andrew Sandel, the office of pastor in the church of Pennsylvania is become vacant, we have appointed for the same our well-beloved Master in Philosophy, Jonas Lidman, ordering all concerned to act accordingly.

"Stockholm, 2d of May, 1719."

With Mr. Lidman, or about the same time, came the Rev. Samuel Hesselius. We find them both present at a meeting of the congregation on the first Sunday in Advent, (about the first of December,) 1719, and also the Rev. Andrew Hesselius, of Christina. On that occasion the above letter of the queen, announcing the appointment of Mr. Lidman to the Wicaco Church, was read; and also letters from Bishop Swedburg to the Swedish congregations in general, and to the church Gloria Dei in particular. The bishop had, on the recall of Mr.

Sandel, recommended Mr. Hesselius as his successor, who was accordingly appointed by the king, with Mr. Lidman as assistant in all the congregations, to aid where most wanted, and to succeed in any that might become vacant; but afterwards he had respectfully advised the queen to appoint Lidman as ordinary pastor, because he had taken the degree of Master in Philosophy, allowing Hesselius to be pastor extraordinary of the church, and assistant to the other churches. The congregations promised their best endeavors to support both pastors.

1720. A meeting was held on the 27th of March, for the transaction of business, at which four clergymen were present: the Rev. Provost Andrew Hesselius, the Rev. Mr. Lidenius, of Racoon and Penn's Neck, and the Rev. Messrs. Lidman and Samuel Hesselius. The provost proposed that the last named clergyman should take charge of those portions of the congregation residing at Kalkonhook and Neshamani. This was objected to by the lay members present, upon the ground that the Swedes living in those places might thus become "weaned" from the mother church at Wicaco. It being understood that one clergyman was competent to the duties at Wicaco, it was then proposed by Mr. Lidman, that as the people at Manating* were

*Supposed to be Morlatton, or Douglasville, four miles above Pottstown, on the Schuylkill, where there was a settlement of Swedes.

at a great distance from the church, they, perhaps, would be glad of his services there, and that he would cheerfully relinquish to him so much of his salary as was furnished by that part of the congregation. Marcus Hulings,* and other "respectable" inhabitants of that part of the country then present, earnestly seconded this proposition, promising to contribute, to the extent of their means, towards his support. It was accordingly arranged that the Rev. Samuel Hesselius should settle at Manating.

At the annual meeting in 1722, the same clergymen were present, with the exception of the Rev. Samuel Hesselius. At this meeting "the provost preached an excellent sermon on the duties of ministers and parishioners, to live in reciprocal concord, and by faithful co-operation to promote the kingdom of Christ on earth." The subject of providing a Swedish School for children was considered, but there being some difficulties in the way, it was concluded that they "would themselves instruct their children, after they had learned to read English."

In 1723 Mr. Lidman complained of the insufficiency of his salary to his support, and wished to receive some benefit from the church land at Wicaco. It was resolved to fence it, to

* This Marcus Hulings was my great-grandfather, his daughter Magdalena, having married Matthias Holstein, my grandfather.

divide the part lying between the Moyamensing and Passyunk roads into two parts, and to let them as pasture grounds; but "to reserve seventy trees for the use of the congregation." Two years afterwards it was resolved "to let the pasture ground next to the church, to some honest person, for the relief of the pastor."

In 1725, it was proposed by Mr. Lidman immediately to repair the church roof on the south side, which was quite decayed. The congregation promised attention to it. Two years afterwards, (1727,) we find the outer doors and pews requiring speedy repairs. The next year the same thing was advised of "the windows and shutters of the church."

In 1730, the Rev. Mr. Lidman informed the congregation that he had received a letter from Bishop Swedburg, notifying him of his recall by the king, and his appointment to a "good parish in Sweden." He suggested the propriety of "presenting by him to the king, and to Bishop Swedburg, some articles of peltry, as marks of gratitude for the favors received." To which the congregation cheerfully agreed. He preached his farewell sermon on the twenty-fourth Sunday after Trinity.

The Rev. J. Eneberg was appointed to fill the vacancy until a pastor could be procured from Sweden.

In 1731, the glebe in Passyunk was leased

to Peter Cock and Mouns Cock, for four pounds yearly.

In 1732, part of the church roof was blown off. Boarding was procured in the city for the clergyman, until a house should be built at Wicaco.

It was agreed that any person in the country who might want the minister's attendance, should furnish a conveyance, as his keeping a horse in town would be troublesome and expensive.

1733. On the seventh of January, the first Sunday after Epiphany, the Rev. Gabriel Falck first appeared before the congregation. The Rev. Mr. Eneberg preached. After the service he read Mr. Falck's commission from King Frederick, dated Stockholm, 9th August, 1732; also a letter of recommendation from Bishop Swedburg. This connection of Mr. Falck with Wicaco was dissolved the same year it commenced. What led to the dissolution the records do not show. I have seen it elsewhere stated that he was deposed. The congregation immediately applied for a successor, but the letter was never received. Another letter was written in 1736; in answer to which the Rev. John Dylander was appointed to the rectorship. He arrived in Philadelphia on the 2d of November, 1737, and preached his first sermon on the 6th of the same month "to a very large congregation." After service the Rev. Mr.

Tranberg, pastor of the Racoon and Penn's Neck churches, read the King's commission, dated Stockholm, 27th May, 1737, and also the letters of the venerable Consistory* of Upsala to the congregation, dated 8th January, 1737, signed by the Archbishop Johannes Steuchius, and four members of the consistory, viz. Olof Celsius, E. Melander, Andreas Winborn, and John Wisman.

The Archbishop made known in his letter that he had been appointed by the king super-

*We have reference frequently made, in Swedish Ecclesiastical affairs, to the "Consistory of Upsala." From the epithet "venerable," here applied to it, its authority would seem to have been of long standing. The first mention I find made of the Consistory occurs in the reign of Gustavus Adolphus, in 1623 and 1625. In the first of these years, the king proposed that there should be such a body, to consist of six ecclesiastical, and six lay members, before whom "all complaints regarding cathedral chapters, or other ecclesiastical matters, referred to the king's majesty, and requiring redress, were to be laid." They were also to "watch over purity of doctrine, and to have inspection and censorship over printers and booksellers." The bishops and clergy not liking the *lay* feature in this plan, the king, in 1625, offered a new proposition, according to which the Consistory should "consist properly of ecclesiastics, with some political persons, competent to the office, who should attend on the king's behalf, yet without the right of voting." Neither proposition proved acceptable to the Bishops and others, and in the reign of Queen Christina, the subject was brought forward in some new shape.—*See* HISTORY OF THE SWEDES, *by Geijer, Historiographer Royal of Sweden, etc.; pp.* 233–234. *Translated by J. H. Turner, Esq.*

intendent of the Swedish mission, in the place of Bishop Swedburg, deceased; and that at his request the consistory were added, that they might, in the event of his death, execute the trust. He assured the congregation of his best endeavors to promote their spiritual welfare.

The parsonage house at Wicaco was built in 1733.

At a meeting of the congregation, held on the 25th of November, 1737, the wardens, among other duties to which their attention was called, were reminded that they were expected to "admonish parents to instruct their children in religious principles, to practise domestic devotion, by morning and evening prayers; to reprove those who lead a bad life, in idleness, ebriety, discord, swearing, neglect of the divine word and sacraments," etc.

At the same meeting it was reported, that Jacob Bengtson had leased the two lots at Wicaco for £7 10*s*. per annum; and that Andrew Rambo had leased the glebe in Passyunk for £5 per annum.

In the spring of 1738, the Swedish members at Kalkonhook (below Darby) wished to build a church there, for their greater convenience in attending divine worship, and solicited assistance from the members at Wicaco; which the latter promised to give the following year, when a suitable place for the church should have been chosen. The design fell through at that time.

In the fall of 1738, expensive repairs to the church were found necessary.

The congregation lost the Rev. Mr. Dylander by death, after he had been with them four years. He died on the 2d of November, 1741. He appears to have possessed great vocal powers, and to have delighted his hearers with the sweetness of his music. His remains were interred beneath the chancel at Wicaco, and are covered by a marble slab, with the following inscription:

"In memory of the Rev. JOHN DYLANDER, missionary from Sweden, and four years minister of this church, who died November 2, 1741, Ætatis suæ, 32.

"While here he sang his Maker's praise,
The listening angels heard his song,
And called their consort soul away,
Pleased with a strain so like their own.

"His soul attentive to the call,
And quickly listening to obey,
Soared to ethereal scenes of bliss,
Too pure to dwell in grosser clay."

The Rev. Gabriel Nesman was appointed to succeed the Rev. Mr. Dylander. He arrived in Philadelphia on the 20th of October, 1743. The vacancy in the pulpit of four years between Mr. Falck's and Mr. Dylander's ministrations;

and of two years between the death of the latter, and the arrival of Mr. Nesman, had an injurious effect upon the interests of the church. For want of a pastor in their own church, many of the Swedes attached themselves to other churches, some going to "English churches," and others being led away by the eloquence of Mr. Whitfield. Mr. Nesman deplored this state of things, and did all in his power to revive towards their own church the languishing zeal of the Swedes. He also took an early opportunity of calling the attention of parents to the early baptism of their children, and to the propriety of this ordinance being administered as often as possible in the church, and not in private houses.

I find the following entry in relation to persons not regularly receiving the Lord's Supper. "Persons not communicating twice a year, must be admonished, first by the pastor alone, and if regardless, again by him and the elders of the parish; and if they still neglect, shall forfeit the right of voting at the meetings of the congregation. Those who seldom or never perform this Christian duty, and disregard faithful warnings, shall be disowned, both by the pastor and congregation, and he shall not cultivate friendship with them."

Another entry: "Whereas, the kings of Sweden have, from the first colonization to the present time, graciously favored the congregations with Swedish clergymen, gratitude and prudence require us not to choose any in case of a vacancy, but wait for the arrival of a successor, duly qualified by clerical ordination, and royal commission; and in the mean time be contented with the aid that ministers of the other congregations can give."

Mr. Nesman brought over a fresh supply of Swedish books for the use of the different churches.

1744. At the election for wardens and vestrymen this year, Jacob Bengtson, Peter Jones, and Andrew Toy, were chosen in the place of Benjamin Bengtson, Martin Garrets, and Lars Bure, who, on account of advanced age, wished to resign. In accepting their resignation, it was provided "that they should retain the privilege of voting with the new trustees on all occasions." The other members of the vestry were, Peter Cock, merchant in Philadelphia, and a native of Sweden; Hans Tate, and Jacob Archer, both of Amasland. John Henderson, of the latter place, resigned the wardenship, and Andrew Georgen was appointed in his place.

1745. The wardens and vestrymen this year were, Andrew Bonde, John Garret, Jacob Bengtson, Elias Rambo, wardens; and Charles Grantham, Jacob Rambo, Andrew Justis, Morton Morton, vestrymen.

1747. A resolution was passed to shingle the

north side of the church roof. It was done the following year.

1750. By a letter dated the 22d of February, this year, the Archbishop (Benzelius) informed the Rev. Mr. Nesman of his recall to Sweden, and of the appointment of the Rev. Olof Parlin, as his successor. Mr. Parlin arrived in the ship Speedwell, Captain Nicholas Stevenson, on the 7th of July, and was "very kindly received by the trustees and members residing in the city," and afterwards with the same cordiality by those living in the country. He preached his first sermon on the 22d of July, the sixth Sunday after Trinity, from Jeremiah i. 7: "Thou shalt go to all that I shall send thee, and whatsoever I command thee thou shalt speak." The provost, Rev. Israel Acrelius, and rector of Christina, also preached from Matthew ix. 37, 38: "The harvest truly is plenteous, but the laborers are few; pray ye therefore the Lord of the harvest, that he will send forth laborers into the harvest." On this occasion the Rev. Mr. Nesman, and the Rev. Eric Unander, assistant minister of the mission, introduced the new rector, whose commission from King Frederick, and the letters of the Archbishop, and the members of the Consistory, were read to the congregation by the Rev. Mr. Unander. In these letters the congregations were urged to continue steadfast in their religious principles, and gratefully to remember the interest taken in their spiritual welfare by the kings of Sweden, in sending them worthy ministers, the expenses of whose voyages they paid, etc.

1757. In the spring of this year, the Rev. Eric Norderlind was appointed assistant minister to Mr. Parlin, to officiate "in all the congregations." On the 22d of December, of the same year, Mr. Parlin died, of pleurisy, after an illness of four days. His remains lie beneath the chancel of Wicaco church, by the side of his predecessors, Rudman and Dylander. On the stone which covers his grave is a Latin inscription, expressive of the learning, piety, etc., of him whose name it records. He appears to have been generally respected and esteemed, as his funeral was attended by "a great number of various religious denominations." The Rev. Mr. Unander, of Christina, preached on the occasion in English; and on the 26th, the Rev. Mr. Lidenius in Swedish from 2 Timothy, iv. 6, 7, 8: "For I am now ready to be offered," etc.

The following is the inscription on the stone over his grave:

"Siste, viator, quisque et mortalis, funde lachrymas in hoc corruptionis domicilio. Jacet in pace et quiete, beate mortuus, vir eruditione conspicuus, a Deo doctus, plur. reverendus, Dus. magister Olavus Parlin, Ecclesiarum Sueco-Lutherarum, quæ Deo colliguntur in Boreali America, prœpositus et pastor in Wicacoa meritissimus. Natus Suecæ, A. D. MDCCXVI, ordinatus Verbi Divini minister, A. D. MDCCXLV. Adiit Americam 1750, inivit societatem conjugalem 1751, obiit die 22 Decem. A°. 1757.

"He was an affectionate husband, a tender father, a true friend, and during his christian warfare, a faithful and valiant soldier of Jesus Christ; and in the last combat, strengthened by heavenly succours, he quitted the field, not captive, but conqueror, and is numbered among the children of God."

Translation of the Latin:

"Stop, traveller, who art thyself mortal, and drop a tear upon this receptacle of corruption. Here lies quietly and in peace, after a happy death, a man conspicuous in erudition, taught of God, the most reverend, most learned Olof Parlin, Provost of the Swedish-Lutheran churches which are collected by God in North America, and placed as most worthy pastor over that in Wicacoa. He was born in Sweden, A. D., 1716, ordained minister of the Divine Word, A. D., 1745, came to America in 1750, was married in 1751, and died December 22, 1757."

Under the chancel floor is another stone, containing the following inscription:

"Siste, viator, ingemisce mortalium fatis. Petrus Kock, Suecus, qui Borealis oritur D. XVIII ante Calend. Dec., A. R. S., **CIƆIƆCCIIII**, et in occidente occidit D. IIII ante Idus Septem. A. **CIƆIƆCCXXXXVIIII.** Disce omnia in hoc orbe ad occasum vergere."

Translated thus:

"Stop, traveller, mourn over the fate of mortals. Peter Kock, a Swede, born at the north on the 18th day before the Calends of December in the year 1704, died in the west the fourth day before the Ides of September, in the year 1749. Learn that all things in this world tend to death.

"If in this life only, we have hope in Christ, we are of all men most miserable; but thanks be to God," etc.—1 *Cor.* xv.

I may as well mention in this place, that under what was formerly the central aisle, are two stones, bearing the following inscriptions:

"Here lieth the remains of MAGDALEN ROBESON, eldest daughter of the late Rev. Andrew Rudman, commissary of the Swedish Mission; born 24 February, A. D., 1699, married to Mr. Andrew Robeson, A. D. 1718, and after his death, A. D. 1740, continued during the remainder of her life a widow indeed. Died 25 February, 1769, aged 70 years."

"In memory of ELIZABETH VANDERSPIEGEL, widow of William Vanderspiegel, late of the city of Philadelphia, merchant; daughter of the late Andrew and Magdalen Robeson, and granddaughter of the Rev. Andrew Rudman, died 23 February 1774, aged 52 years."

The oldest stone in the yard has the following:

"Here lyeth the body of PETER, the son of Andreas Sandel, minister of this church, who dyed April ye 21, A. D. 1708, aged 2 years and 4 months."

"Here also lyeth the body of ANDREAS, son of Andreas Sandel, who died August 13, A. D. 1711, aged 2 weeks and 2 days."

The remains of Alexander Wilson, the Ornithologist, lie in this yard. The stone that covers his grave has the following inscription:

"This monument covers the remains of
ALEXANDER WILSON,
Author of the AMERICAN ORNITHOLOGY,
He was born in Renfrewshire, Scotland, on 6th July, 1766,
Emigrated to the United States, 1794,
And died in Philad'a, of Dysentery on the 23 Aug., 1813,
AGED 47.
Ingenio stat sine morte decus."

CHAPTER IX.

By a letter dated 2d of January, 1758, the archbishop and consistory of Upsal, were notified of the death of Mr. Parlin, and that Mr. Norderlind would supply the church during the vacancy. They also requested that the widow and two small children of their late rector might be recommended to some relief. In applying for a successor to Mr. Parlin, the congregation desired that their pastor might in future be permitted to preach occasionally in English, the Swedes and English becoming so intermixed as to render necessary religious instruction in both languages.

1759. The Rev. Mr. Norderlind continued to officiate for the Swedes until the spring of this year, when the Rev. Charles Magnus Wrangel arrived and took charge of the church. It was in his time, or about 1763, that the churches at Kingsessing and Upper Merion were built. He was one of the most popular preachers the Swedes ever had among them, and was usually obliged, on account of the crowds who attended his ministry, to preach in the open air. I have heard him represented as possesing a most wining and captivating eloquence. He returned to Sweden in 1768, and was there made a bishop. He died in 1786.

The Rev. Andrew Goeranson, who was sent over in 1766, entered upon the duties of his office as rector, in the spring or summer of 1768. He contiued to officiate until the close of the year 1779. He returned home in 1785, and died in 1800.

1780. The Rev. Matthias Hultgren took charge of the church in January of this year, and continued to officiate as rector until the spring of 1786, his last baptism having been on the 30th of May of that year.

1786. In July of this year, the Rev. Dr. Nicholas Collin, who was sent over in 1770, and had been for some time officiating at Swedesborough, New Jersey, was appointed rector of Wicaco and churches in connection. He presided over these for a period of forty-five years; in which time he married three thousand three hundred and seventy-five couples, averaging about eighty-four couples a year. In the early part of his ministry it averaged much more than this. The number of couples married by him in 1795 was one hundred and ninety-nine, and in the following year one hundred and seventy-nine.

Dr. Collin, during the whole period of his ministry, was held in high respect by his congregations.* He possessed considerable learning, particularly in an acquaintance with languages. The only work which he has left behind him is a manuscript translation of Acrelius' History of New Sweden, which he undertook in 1799, at the request of the Historical Society of New York, in whose possession it now is. He was a member, and for some time one of the vice presidents, of the American Philosophical Society. And was also one of the eighteen founders of the Society "for the commemoration of the landing of William Penn." He died at Wicaco, on the 7th of October, A. D. 1831, in the eighty-seventh year of his age.

The Rev. Dr. Collin has given, in the records of the church at Swedesborough, the following "brief account of the Swedish Mission from its

* To show the mistakes often made by foreigners in speaking of this country, the following extract is here given from a late number of the Foreign Quarterly Review, under the caption of "Swedish Periodical Literature." The Review, speaking of the clergy sent from Sweden to supply the spiritual wants of their colony on the Delaware, has these remarks:—One of those then in America, Mr. Collin, preferred to remain in the colony, where the pension, to which he would have been entitled on his return home was, in the year 1825, still paid him from Sweden; and so highly satisfactory does his determination of remaining appear to have been, not merely to his flock, but to all who knew him, that he has since, although a native Swede, *had the honor of being elected one of the representatives of Pennsylvania in Congress.*"

commencement to its termination." It is a document which has never before been published. We present it to the reader as corroborative of many of the statements contained in this book; as furnishing us with some new facts; and because we think it will be gratifying to the many friends of the Doctor still living, to read the result of his inquiries and experience in regard to the interesting mission in which he so long occupied a prominent position, and which his death brought to a final close.

DR. COLLIN'S NARRATIVE.

"The first Swedish Colony in North America arrived in the year 1634, and was followed by three or four reinforcements during the succeeding years up to 1654. The Swedes acquired, by a fair purchase from the natives, all the western shore of the Delaware, from Cape Henlopen to Trenton, and extending due west to a distance of forty miles. Their first principal settlement was at Christina creek, where they had a considerable fort, and a church. After some years their establishments extended along the river forty or fifty miles beyond Philadelphia, and they had a church at Tinicum, where also the governor resided. The Low Dutch had, some time before the arrival of the Swedes, taken possession of North river, and founded New Amsterdam, now New York.

N. Collin

They had also gotten a slender footing on the eastern shore of the Delaware, and built a fort called Nassau, where Gloucester now is. This vicinity naturally created jealousy, which produced contest, and finally hostilities, that terminated in the conquest of the infant Swedish colony, as it was not supported by Sweden, which was at that time engaged in war with several of the first powers in Europe.

"After the death of those clergymen who accompanied the first colonists from Sweden, the people became very destitute until, on their humble address to Charles XI. King of Sweden, the mission was instituted, which has continued without intermission to this time. The mission was composed of three distinct rectorships, viz. Wicaco, with Kingsessing and Upper Merion, in Pennsylvania; Christina, in Delaware; and Racoon, with Penn's Neck, in West Jersey. The clergy consisted of the three respective rectors, and in later times a minister extraordinary, or common assistant. One of the ordinary pastors was also provost, or commissary, having a degree of superintending authority over the whole mission. The minister extraordinary had from Sweden a yearly salary of £33⅓ sterling. The commissary office has had, from the time of Mr. Sandin, £50. The crown gave to every coming missionary £50 sterling, to defray the expenses of the voyage, and an equal sum on returning. While waiting for preferment after their return, they had adequate pensions; the commissaries one-third more than the others. They also obtained very good employments, several having been rewarded with the best rectorships in Sweden.

"Until the beginning of this century, Racoon and Penn's Neck made parts of the congregations over the river, or on the Pennsylvania side: the first of Wicaco, and the other of Christina. In the year 1704, a church was built where the present church of Swedesborough now stands, and was endowed with the lands yet preserved, viz. the hundred acres, of which Swedesborough makes a part, and the marsh meadow of six acres, four miles from thence down Racoon creek. Their first minister, Polfladius, was drowned in Delaware, A. D. 1706. The second, Mr. Auren, died A. D. 1713. He was succeeded by Abraham Lidenius, who also became pastor of Penn's Neck. A church was erected there in A. D. 1717, and by Yagnet endowed with four acres of land. From that time both congregations have been united, and both conjoined in the commissions of the rectors.

"By the unwearied solicitude of Mr. Lidenius, the congregations were, after eight years consultation, prevailed upon to purchase the glebe in Pilesgrove, which contains two hundred and thirty-five acres, and cost one hundred and forty-five pounds. In 1724, Mr. Lidenius went home to Sweden, with his wife, Maria Van Neaman, and three children.

"Peter Tranberg arrived in 1726, with Andrew Windrufwa, who, as assistant, had charge of Penn's Neck until 1728, when he died. In 1741, Mr. Tranberg was promoted to the rectorship of Christina, where he died. This vacancy was in some measure supplied by William Malander. This person had come to America with Dylander, pastor of Wicaco, as schoolmaster. Being a student of divinity, he obtained permission to preach and baptize children, and would, by a mandate* of the archbishop, have received holy orders from the said Dylander and Tranberg, if the first-mentioned had not, in the meantime, departed this life. During the vacancy the Moravians created a schism, and built the meeting house on Oldman's creek. Pastor Naesman, from Wicaco, and Mr. Tranberg, from Christina, did, however, occasionally supply the congregations.

"The Rev. John Sandin arrived the first of April, A. D. 1748, with his wife and a young child, after a tedious and perilous voyage. He died after six months. Professor Kalm, who at this time, by the king of Sweden's order, travelled through North America, resided for the winter at Racoon, and preached in the

*It was no doubt under such mandate that Mr. Falkner was ordained—*page* 78.

church. He afterwards married Mrs. Sandin, and went with her to Sweden, encountering on the passage a tremendous tempest.
tina church, and afterwards went home. John

"Eric Unander, who came in as minister extraordinary, became in 1751, pastor of the two churches. In 1756 he was promoted to Chris-
Abraham Lidenius, son of the above mentioned Lidenius, succeeded as rector, after having, since 1751, served as assistant in these congregations and those of Pennsylvania. He obtained his recall, but in the meantime died in Pennsylvania. His successor, the Rev. John Wicsell, became rector A. D. 1762. His active zeal for the spiritual and temporal concerns of the congregations is yet remembered. By his exertions the parsonage house in Swedesborough was erected, the lot leased, the marsh meadow banked and tussucked, and the swamp near Swedesborough cleared out for pasture. He has also the principal credit for the charity school house in Swedesborough. In autumn, 1773, he returned, and was promoted to the important rectorship of Munklofp, in the central part of Sweden, where he is yet living, (1786.) He was provost, or commissary, for the mission during two years.

"Nicholas Collin arrived in 1770, the 12th of May, as minister extraordinary, and officiated through the mission, but especially at Racoon and Penn's Neck, until the departure of Mr. Wicsell. Since that time, until July, 1786, he was rector of these congregations, and for seven years provost of the mission. By letters to the archbishop and consistory of Upsal, dated 8th July, 1778, I solicited, in pressing terms, for my recall. I had then officiated for above eight years within the mission, and was consequently entitled to preferment at home. There was, moreover, a strong necessity for departure. The rents of the church lands had, by the depreciation of the current money, and the dearness of many necessary articles, fallen to a tenth part of their usual value. The congregations had suffered great distress from the war; and many of the more able members were, as is common in America, unwilling to contribute for the support of public worship. There was no prospect of peace or civil order for several years; and consequently no hopes of relief. A temporary vacancy, though prejudicial to the congregations, was therefore inevitable: at the same time a saving of the little church revenue after my departure, would shorten this vacancy by adding to the support of my successor. All this was fully represented in the above-mentioned letter, with an express declaration that, without a speedy alleviation of my sufferings, I should not even wait for the recall, but depart in the following spring. It must be observed, that my want of subsistence would not have been grievous if I could have drawn my commissary salary: but this was impracticable, as all communication with Sweden was cut off by the dreadful disorders of those times. When the seat of war was removed from the Delaware, I obtained, at least, more tranquility, and therefore resolved to wait for my recall, repeating my solicitation by several letters for two years. My request was at last granted, by the king's resolve of 22d November, A. D. 1782. The reason of this delay was that the consistory had not sooner presented my petition, because his majesty had, by a previous order, signified his pleasure that the American missionaries should remain in their stations until the event of the war was known. In May, 1783, I received this recall. I should then with pleasure have returned to my dear native country, but personal concerns, and anxiety for my ecclesiastical trust, determined me to still continue for some time; especially as the urgent plea of necessity had now ceased with the return of peace. I therefore informed the consistory of my resolution to remain for a short period, until the congregations should be supplied with a successor; declaring also that in case the king was pleased to continue the mission, I was willing to take upon me the charge of Wicaco, Kingsessing and Upper Merion, which churches were becoming vacant by the recall of the Rev. Matthias Hultgren; as a new comer, however deserving, could not be useful in that station because of the extinction of the Swedish language. I also expressed my readiness to assist my successor in Racoon and Penn's Neck, by all the influence I derived from long service and personal connections.

"On this request his majesty was pleased, by resolve of the 10th August, 1785, to appoint me rector of those congregations, and also to leave Racoon and Penn's Neck vacant, until they should express their option of the king's future regulation for the Swedish Mission. This was—'That whereas the congregations in their present mature state must be sufficiently able to support their ministers; and whereas they had nearly lost the language of their ancestors, which was a principal tie of their connection with Sweden; therefore, the congregations could not in future obtain any ministers from Sweden without a formal stipulation to defray the whole expenses of the voyage, coming and returning, and to afford them a decent support during their continuance in the ministry.' The king was pleased to add, that future ministers, who might choose to go upon these terms, should not be entitled to the superior privileges of pension and preferments heretofore granted to the American missionaries.

"The congregations of Racoon and Penn's Neck, yet feeling the disasters of a calamitous war, and the first being moreover involved in a most difficult enterprise of erecting the new church, could not immediately comply with these conditions. I therefore informed the archbishop that for the present a temporary vacancy was eligible, and that I would, to the utmost of my power, lessen the disadvantages thereof.

"It must be remarked that the Swedish government had already, in the year 1773, by the ministry of the mission, proposed to the respective congregations, a partial reform of the former plan, to wit: that they should bear the expenses of the voyage from London to America, and from here again to that place, for their pastors, the crown, as usual, defraying the remaining part. The intervening war prevented any attention to this proposal. It was laid before the respective vestries on the restoration of peace. Those of Wicaco, with its annexes, and of Christina, resolved to comply with the demand, in case they should request the favor of Swedish successors after their present pastors. That of Racoon and Penn's Neck promised to contribute according to the ability of the less opulent congregations.

"In the meantime the Swedish language decreased continually, by decease of the ancient people. The clergy themselves were sensible of the great disadvantages attending the usual change of missionaries every seventh or eighth year; and represented the matter in its true light to the archbishop and consistory. The vestry of Wicaco, Kingsessing and Upper Merion received with grateful respect my appointment to their churches, and acknowledged their great obligation to the king of Sweden and his illustrious predecessors, for the long continued care of their spiritual welfare, but at the same time declined a continuance of this favor, as the great change of circumstances must hereafter make the mission a burden to the crown of Sweden, without an adequate benefit to the congragations, which had totally lost the language of their ancestors. They therefore signified their intention of providing for themselves after my departure. The vestry of Christina church expressed the same sentiments. The congregations of Racoon and Penn's Neck did not come to an immediate resolution on this affair, but by my advice waited until the debt incurred for the new church was somewhat reduced, by the rents falling due after my removal, and in the view of knowing how long the mission might be kept up in the other churches under the Rev. Lawrence Girelius and myself. The daily decay of the Swedish tongue, by the death of ancient and respectable members; the probability of our speedy return to Sweden; the unpleasant situation of a solitary missionary, and the great expense of a probably frequent change of ministers, insupportable for the small revenue of their churches, finally determined their coincidence in sentiment with their sister congregations.

"The archbishop of Sweden, having submitted to his majesty these sentiments of the congregations, received the king's final resolve, which he communicated in a letter addressed to the vestries of the churches that composed the mission, dated Upsal, 25th June, 1789; of which the following is the principal matter, accurately translated:

"'The King, approving of the reasons that induce the congregations henceforth to choose their own ministers, rather than to be supplied with Swedish missionaries at the expense of the Swedish crown, has thereunto given his gracious consent, and in consequence thereof permits the yet remaining Swedish missionaries, the commissaries, Lawrence Girelius and Nicholas Collin, to return to their native country, as soon as their circumstances may render it convenient. At the same time, the king from the love he bears to the Swedish name, apprecates unto all the members of these congregations, as in great part descendants from Sweden, all manner of felicity, spiritual and temporal; and will have them assured of his royal favor. It shall also ever be my sincere wish and ardent prayer, that Almighty God may, with his grace and mercies, embrace the members of these congregations, jointly and separately, and that the gospel light which was first kindled in those parts by the tender solicitude of Swedish kings, and the zeal of Swedish clergymen, may there, while days are numbered, shine with perfect brightness, and produce the most salutary fruits.

"'The grace of our Lord Jesus Christ, the love of the Father, and the fellowship of the Holy Ghost, be with, and over you all, wishes from a most sincere heart.

Your affectionate servant,

UNO VON TROIL.'

"During the vacancy I gave the congregations every attention consistent with my distant situation and multiplicity of business. At Swedesborough I performed divine service every third Sunday during the summer and autumn of 1786; and by longer intervals the two following years. I likewise visited some worthy members in their sickness; and preached some funeral sermons. Besides, I made frequent journeys for settling the business of the new church. Penn's Neck could not possibly obtain the same share of service, yet I officiated for a few times at that church, and also preached occasionally at houses on afternoons, after finishing the service at Racoon.

"Having no doubt but that the Swedish government would take the above final resolution upon the mission, I consulted with the vestry on the means of providing an American successor. We determined to make proposals to the Rev. Christian Street, pastor of a Lutheran church in Virginia. He paid a visit to Swedesborough in the fall of 1788, and expressed great satisfaction in the honor conferred upon him—desiring some time for consideration. By letter of the 1st September, 1789, he notified that he must with regret decline the offer, because of a precarious state of health, and the impossibility of providing a successor in his congregations.* This gentleman had been educated by Dr. Wrangel, when rector of Wicaco, and afterwards ordained by the German Lutheran ministry. With a knowledge of the German tongue, he has, being country born, a perfect expression in the English.

"After failing in this, I intended to try other means for an auspicious settlement of the churches. In the meantime, the vestry of Swedesborough engaged the Rev. Mr. Croes† to give what service he could, and after a few months' satisfactory trial called him to the pastoral charge: which I hope and sincerely pray may promote the glory of God, and the happiness of souls.

"In the mean time, Mr. Wade‡ had, for a

*German.

†Of the Episcopal Church, and afterwards Bishop of New Jersey.—Ed.

‡Also an Episcopal Clergyman.

twelve-month, served the congregation, by agreement between him and them, without any interposition of mine.

"The foregoing narrative sufficiently accounts for the gradual cessation of the Swedish mission; first in Racoon and Penn's Neck, and afterwards in the Christina church, by the return of Dr.* Girelius to Sweden in the month of May last, with his wife and four children.

"Every person of reflection must be sensible that the Swedish mission has in a considerable degree contributed to the moral civilization of this young country. This great blessing claims the more gratitude from all concerned, as the kindness of their mother country was perfectly gratuitous, and yet very troublesome. The total expense of the mission, for near a century, amounted to seven or eight thousand pounds sterling. The missionaries have encountered great hardships by long and perilous voyages; many years absence from a land peculiarly dear to Swedes; by the indigent circumstances of a new country, and by the difficulties of a clerical charge where the interest of religion is not supported either by law or public opinion. The pastors of Racoon and Penn's Neck have always borne the heaviest burden, from the insalubrity of a low,

* The Doctorate was conferred by the University of Pennsylvania.

swampy and less improved country;* the scattered situation of the people for thirty miles in length and twelve in breadth, and from the scantiness of support, the revenue of the church lands being small, and ministers never having any regular salaries, but depending on the presents of a few generous members. My sufferings have been very severe. During the war the rents of the church lands were insignificant, by the incredible depreciation of the congress money, which finally passed one hundred and fifty to one specie dollar, and sunk in the hands of the unfortunate holders. The congregations did but little for my relief, because several of the best members were distressed by the barbarous devastations of parties. From these causes, and from the failure of supplies from home, I was at times in want of necessaries. Yet this indigence, however disagreeable to persons accustomed to the conveniences of life, and placed in respectable stations, would have been very supportable in a firm state of health. But, unfortunately, my constitution, already in the second year after my arrival much injured by the fever and ague, was every year harassed by various painful disorders, and finally so reduced that a change of place or the grave seemed to be the only alternatives;

* The Swedes had been settled forty years on the western shore of the Delaware before they began to improve the Jersey shore.

especially as I could not, as a Swedish missionary, have relinquished the fatiguing charge of Penn's Neck.

"May divine grace enable the pastors of souls in every nation to approve themselves in all things as ministers of God; 'in much patience, in afflictions, in necessities, in distresses, in imprisonments, in tumults, in labors, in watchings, in fastings, by pureness, by knowledge, by long suffering, by kindness, by love unfeigned, by the word of truth, by the power of God, by the armor of righteousness on the right hand and on the left,' 2 *Cor.* 6; 'then shall they turn many to righteousness, and shine as stars forever,' *Dan.* 12. May the incorruptible seed which Swedish missionaries have sown in these congregations, some times with joy and sometimes with tears, produce abundant fruit of the Spirit, in all goodness, righteousness, and truth, (*Ephes.* 5,) and flourish an eternal, glorious planting in the land of the living.

(Signed,)

NICHOLAS COLLIN,

Late Rector of Racoon and Penn's Neck, and Provost of Swedish Mission, yet Rector of Swedish Churches in Penna.

"Philadelphia, December 10, 1791."

CHAPTER X.

At the time Dr. Collin received his appointment as rector of these churches, the Swedes began to feel the necessity, from the little knowledge of the Swedish language remaining among them, of having clergymen set over them who had received their education in this country. This will appear from the following record of the proceedings of the vestry, in 1786, in relation to Dr. Collin's appointment:* "Whereupon the vestry do agree to receive the Rev. Dr. Collin as their minister: but at the same time reserving to themselves the right of making any new appointment hereafter, as shall be found more useful and beneficial to the said congregations of Wicaco, Kingsessing and Upper Merion. And the Wardens of Wicaco Church are authorized and required to write to the archbishop of Upsal, to desire him to thank his majesty of Sweden in the name of the congregations, for his care and attention towards them heretofore, and in the present instance. But as the said congregations will be better suited (the Swedish language being

*The foregoing statement of Dr. Collin also shows it.

extinct) by the appointment of some suitable minister from this side of the water, and as the Rev. Mr. Collin has expressed a desire of returning to his native country shortly; whenever his majesty of Sweden shall think it proper and convenient to grant him his recall, *the mission to these congregations will undoubtedly cease.*"

It was not surprising therefore, when the vestry, after the death of Dr. Collin, "proceeded to consider what measures it would be proper and necessary to pursue, in order to supply the existing vacancy in the rectorship," that they should have "unanimously adopted the following resolutions:

"First. That the church wardens and vestrymen are of opinion that the mission from Sweden ceased upon the death of their late rector, the Rev. Nicholas Collin.

"Second. That a meeting of the congregation shall be held in the church at Wicaco, on Monday, the 14th day of November. A. D. 1831, at 12 o'clock, noon, for the purposes specified in the fifth section* of the act to confirm and

*"Sec. 5. And whereas it is represented to this house that the Swedish language is almost extinct, and in consequence thereof the mission from Sweden may probably cease to be continued, according to the ancient custom and usage. In that case, and not otherwise, the church wardens and vestrymen of the said United Churches, for the time being, shall convene together the congregations of the said United Churches of Wicaco, Kingsessing and Upper Merion,

amend the charter of the United Swedish Churches, passed the 10th of September, 1787.

"Third. That the acting warden cause a notice of the said meeting to be pubished in the United States Gazette and the American Sentinel for three weeks before the time of the meeting, and three times in the Saturday Evening Post."

Proceedings of the Congregational Meeting.

"The congregations of the United Swedish Churches of Wicaco, Kingsessing, and Upper Merion, convened at the church at Wicaco, on Monday, the 14th day of November, 1831, agreeably to public notice.

"On motion, Charles Wheeler, Esq. was chosen chairman, and William Amies, secretary.

by notice given in one or more of the public newspapers in this city, for at least three weeks successively, and a majority of the said congregation so met, (who are descendants of, or intermarried with, the descendants of those ancient Swedes whose names are upon record in the church books of Wicaco,) as donors to, or purchasers of, the lands now held and belonging to the said church, and who have heretofore attached themselves as members of the said United Churches by serving in the office of vestrymen, or attending divine service either by themselves or families, together with a majority of the church wardens or vestrymen, shall establish some rules or regulations for the future choice or election of a rector and other minister or ministers to supply the said churches. *Provided always* that such rector and other ministers shall be in the ministry of the Lutheran or Episcopal Churches, and hold their faith in the doctrine of the same."

"The meeting being organized, Thomas M. Jolly, Esq. offered the following resolutions, which were respectively read and considered, and on motion adopted:

"Resolved by the members of the congregation of the United Swedish Lutheran Churches of Wicaco, Kingsessing and Upper Merion, that the present and all future vacancies in the rectorships shall be supplied as follows:

"First. The members of the congregation shall meet in their respective churches, at such time as the church wardens and vestrymen may appoint, and vote by ballot for a rector.

"Second. The result of the voting in each church shall be certified to the church wardens and vestrymen, by the persons who receive and count the ballots.

"Third. If it shall appear that any candidate has received majorities in all, or in any two of the churches, the church wardens and vestrymen shall declare such candidate duly elected rector.

"Fourth. If no candidate shall have received a majority of votes in more than one church, the church wardens and vestrymen shall elect the rector from the persons who are highest on the several returns.

"Fifth. No person shall be entitled to vote for rector who is not qualified to vote for vestrymen, agreeably to the charter and by-laws of the corporation.

"Sixth. The elections in the several churches shall be conducted under such regulations as the church wardens and vestrymen may prescribe; provided, however, that they shall cause notices of the time of holding an election to be placed upon the doors of each church, and published in two of the Philadelphia, and one of the Norristown papers, at least ten days before the time fixed for such election.

"Resolved, That the assistant ministers for the said United Churches shall be chosen, as heretofore, by the rector, church wardens and vestrymen."

The following resolution was adopted:

"Resolved, That a committee of three persons be appointed, to lay before the wardens and vestrymen of the United Churches of Wicaco, Kingsessing and Upper Merion, the rules and regulations adopted by the members of the said United Churches this day convened for the future choice and election of a rector, and other minister or ministers to supply said churches, agreeably to the fifth section of the supplement to the charter, passed September 10, 1787, to the end that they may sanction or reject the same.

"The chairman being authorized, appointed Thomas M. Jolly, Charles H. Clay, and Edward Ewing, the committee, agreeably to the last resolution, who having performed the duties assigned them, reported, by their chairman

Mr. Jolly, that the wardens and vestrymen approved the rules and regulations adopted by this meeting.

"On motion, the meeting adjourned.

(Signed,)

CHARLES WHEELER, *Chairman.*

WM. AMIES, *Secretary.*"

In pursuance of the above regulations, the Swedish congregations met in their respective churches on the 5th of December, 1831, and chose the compiler of these Annals rector; he having received all the votes (sixteen) given at Wicaco—all but one (thirty-seven) at Kingsessing—and all those (twenty-nine) given at Upper Merion.

CHAPTER XI.

We thus come to the close of the Swedish Mission, which, having had its commencement with the appointment of the Rev. Messrs. Rudman, Biork, and Auren, was continued for a period of more than 130 years, with faithful attention on the part of the church in Sweden, to the spiritual interests of their countrymen and brethren settled on these shores.

The mission embraces, as we have seen, three different localities, viz.: Christina, now Wilmington, in Delaware; Wicaco, now included within the limits of Philadelphia, having Kingsessing, near the Delaware river, six miles below, and Upper Merion, sixteen miles above, on the Schuylkill river, in connection with the mission; and Racoon and Penn's Neck, in New Jersey. All these churches are now (1858) in connection with the Protestant Episcopal Church in these United States. Upper Merion is not yet *formally* in connection, or so as to be represented, through her laity, in the convention of the Episcopal church. But she, like the rest, gave her choice at once, when the Swedish Mission ceased, in favor of an Episcopal clergyman to minister at her altars.

The church at Christina, and that at Racoon and Penn's Neck became connected with the Episcopal Church as early as about 1790. The long life of Dr. Collin continued the churches at Wicaco, Kingsessing, and Upper Merion as Swedish churches, until the close of the year 1831. He, too, however, constantly during his ministry, used the prayer book of the Episcopal church. And the many assistant ministers that he had, during his long rectorship of forty-five years, were always of the same church. After his death, and the choice, as his successor, of the present rector, there was at once, with the universal approval of the congregations, an entire conformity to the doctrine and worship of the Episcopal Church. The Bishop of Pennsylvania, regularly visited, and confirmed in them.

In 1843, the three churches, included in what had been the Wicaco Mission, dissolved their connection by almost unanimous consent, as one coporate body, and were formed into three distinct parishes, each one having its own separate rector. In a short time after, Kingsessing (St. James') and Wicaco (Gloria Dei) churches came formally into union with the Episcopal church in Pennsylvania. At Upper Merion, soon after they became an independent parish, there was an effort made, by a few disaffected persons having little more than a nominal connection with the congregation, to eject the rector and vestry having charge of the church, upon the ground that being of the *Episcopal* church they had no *right* to the position they occupied. It was the object of these persons to change its character from a *Swedish* Lutheran into a *German* Lutheran congregation. To secure this object, a law-suit was instituted and carried on, with considerable bitterness for some months; the result of which was, the defeat of the prosecutors, and the settlement of the question at issue in favor of the defendants, or of the rector and vestry in authority, as being the lawful successors of those who had preceded them. A desire to avoid further agitation, has, no doubt, been the reason why this congregation has not followed the example set her by the other Swedish churches in seeking a closer union with the Episcopal Church.

The question has been sometimes asked: how was it that all these churches, established, as they were, by the Swedish *Lutheran* Church, and presided over for so long a time by ministers ordained in and appointed by that church, should so immediately upon the dissolution of their connection with Sweden, have come into union with the *Protestant Episcopal Church*, rather than into union with the German Lutheran Church, the name and faith of the same great reformer having been adopted by both? The answer to this question is, that while between the Swedish Lutheran and German Lutheran Churches there is no dissimilarity in faith or doctrine, there is much dissimilarity in regard to *order* or government. The Swedish Church, though *Lutheran* in doctrine, is *Episcopal* in government. In accomplishing the work of the reformation in Germany, parity in the ministry was substituted for Episcopacy with its several orders. Not so in Sweden. The reformers there, in adopting the doctrines of the Augsburg Confession, etc. retained Episcopacy. In casting off the doctrinal errors of the Church of Rome, they had no fault to find with her Episcopal regimen. They rejected the former and retained the latter. They retained it not merely in *name*, but, as seems to be well established, in the possession of the true apostolical succession. The church in Denmark, during the reformation, *lost* that succession. It has retained the Episcopal *name or title*, but, as is generally admitted, their bishops, so called, were and are appointed under an authority lacking the true Episcopal character. No man, or body of men, can *give* what they *do not possess*. The Danes, at the time of the reformation, having lost the succession, never had it restored. Their bishops, therefore, are such only in *name*, and not in *reality*.*

*John Wesley, the founder of Methodism, understood this matter well, and therefore remonstrated, in the strongest terms, against any of his followers assuming to themselves the name of Bishop.

But the Swedish Church is Episcopal in *reality* as well as in *name*. We do not make this assertion lightly, but think we have sufficient proof to establish its truth. Much of the learning of Sweden is shut up in a language but little known in other parts of Europe and in our own country. This makes it often difficult to consult their authorities, as there are not many instances in which Swedish works are translated.

In considering the subject of Episcopacy in Sweden, it seems proper to notice briefly the time and manner of the introduction of christianity into that country. We are told by their historians, that in the early part of the ninth century, the Swedes sent messengers to the Emperor, Louis the Pious, announcing that many of their people longed to embrace the christian faith. Anskar, a Frank, who was connected with a convent in Picardy, and was a zealous preacher, had felt from childhood a desire to devote himself to the conversion of the heathen. Him the emperor consulted as to his willingness to undertake the mission among the Swedes. He cheerfully consented to it, and chose as an associate in the same holy undertaking, a pious brother of the same convent named Withmar. He was welcomed by Biorn, the reigning king. He found in those regions christian captives, who had imparted to some extent to the people, the knowledge of christianity. This first journey of Anskar to Sweden was made in 829. The next year was the first of his christian labors among the Swedes. Returning from Sweden, Anskar was appointed to the archbishopric of Hamburg, lately established for the conversion of the north. But this place being soon after destroyed by "the northern sea-kings," he was appointed archbishop of Bremen. From this place he continued the work which he had begun, and when no one else could be found to undertake the laborious and perilous enterprise, revisited Sweden himself in the year 853. A church was founded while he remained, and after he had finally departed, he continued as long as he lived to make provision for supplying the Swedes with instructors. After the death of Anskar in 865, no christian teacher ventured for seventy years to Sweden, and the people seem to have relapsed into idolatry.

Olave, styled the lap-king, was the first monarch of Sweden who embraced christianity. He was baptized by the holy Bishop Sigfrid about the year 1000. This good man had been invited from England by Olave. He was the second apostle of the north. Anskar was the first. Sigfrid devoted a long life to the preaching of christianity among the Swedes.

The first Bishop of Upsala was St. Henry, (anno 1160,) of whose active exertions in propagating christianity, history has left some record. He was the first apostle of the Finns, and suffered among them the death of a martyr. The archbishopric of Upsala was established in the year 1163. The bishops of Skara, Sinkoping, Strengness, Westeras, and shortly afterwards of Wexio and Abo, are mentioned as suffragans of his see. He was himself subordinate to the archbishop of Lund, who bore the title of Primate of Sweden. The archbishopric of Lund was afterwards abrogated.*

It was in 1519 that the doctrines of the Reformation were first preached in Sweden. Olaus and Laurentius Petri, otherwise named Olave and Laurence Peterson, two brothers, who had studied at Wittemburg, and were disciples of Luther, returned in the year just mentioned to ther native country, and entered upon the work of propagating the reformed faith. The king, Gustavus Vasa, was himself in correspondence with Luther, and did all in his power to promote the spread of the Reformation. The bold sermons of Olaus Petri†

*See History of the Swedes, by Eric Gustave Geijer, of which his translator says: "The work possesses a European reputation; all competent judges admit that the writer has added one to the scanty list of great national histories."

†Mosheim, in his Church History, (vol. iv. p. 78,) speaking of the Reformation in Sweden, says, that the King, Gustavus Vasa, "spread abroad through the kingdom the Swedish translation of the bible that had been made by Olaus Petri." He also says that, "in the year 1526, he appointed a conference at Upsal, between this eminent re-

at the elective diet of Strengness, had excited general attention, and the king appointed him minister, etc. of Stockholm, and made his younger brother, Laurentius, professor in Upsala.*

The Reformation was carried on with the same moderation in Sweden that it was in England, the object being to get rid of the *corruptions* that had been introduced into the church, and not to utterly *destroy* it, as having nothing good remaining to it. We are told by Professor Geijer (page 119) that there was "caution used in changing the old observances of the church," and he quotes Olaus Petri as saying in his Swedish Manual, published at that time, that "most of the ceremonies were allowed to stand which had been theretofore used, and *were not contrary to God's word.*" Under the influence of this desire to retain whatever was not contrary to God's word, and especially

former and Peter Gallius, a zealous defender of the ancient superstition, in which these two champions were to plead publicly in behalf of their respective opinions, that it might thus be seen on which side the truth lay. The dispute, in which Olaus obtained a signal victory, contributed much to confirm Gustavus in the persuasion of the truth of Luther's doctrine, and to promote the progress of that doctrine in Sweden."

* He was afterwards (1531) appointed archbishop, and was the first Protestant archbishop of Sweden. He died at an advanced age in 1573. He was succeeded by his son-in-law, Laurentius Petri Gothus, who "was consecrated in 1575, with full hierarchical pomp."

to retain all that was *in agreement* with it, *Episcopacy* was retained and perpetuated in Sweden. Geijer, speaking of the Diet of Westeras, assembled by Gustavus Vasa in 1527, and of the presence there, among other bishops, of Petrus Magni, or, as the translator has it, Peter Magnuson, expressly says, that this Petrus Magni was consecrated at Rome, by the king's special request, and that this bishop so consecrated "*afterwards* consecrated the bishops appointed by the king."*

In agreement with the foregoing is the following article from the "English Churchman." "The Church of Sweden is a daughter of the Church of England. Sigfrid, the first Bishop of Wexio, and Apostle of Sweden, had previously been Archbishop of York, and the mission he headed was the last sent out from England before the Norman conquest. The foundation, permanently, of the Swedish Church may be assigned to A. D. 1000, or thereabouts. The Papal usurpations began to be introduced about forty years after, though with extreme difficulty. In the sixteenth century the Reformation was commenced in the Swedish Church, and consolidated in the synod of Upsala, 1593.

"As the Episcopal succession in Sweden has been doubtfully spoken of by a writer in the *Ecclesiastic* for November, 1852, the follow-

* Page 116, note 3.

ing extract is quoted from the *Svenska Kyrkordnung* of the Rev. Dr. Knos, Professor of Theology in the University of Upsala:

"'That at the introduction of the Reformation the apostolical succession was preserved is an historical fact, fully proved. Even Gustavus I. Vasa, deemed this of such great importance that he had the first Protestant Bishops consecrated in Westeras Cathedral by the bishop Petrus Magni, who had been solemnly consecrated at Rome by a Roman Cardinal. From this Petrus Magni is thus derived this preserved succession, and ever since every Swedish Bishop has been conseceated by a bishop already consecrated in this succession. Moreover, when the attempt was made in the reign of John III. again to Romanize the Swedish Church, the adherents of the see of Rome expressed no doubts as to the rightful Canonical Succession of the Swedish Bishops. The distinct injunctions of all Swedish Church ordinances, that no bishop shall exercise his functions until he be consecrated thereto, and the many records of actual Episcopal consecrations in existence, are the strongest proofs that no change was subsequently introduced in this respect.'"

The following letter, too, of the Rev. Geo. Scott, who resided for some years in Sweden as a Methodist Minister, and which was published in London in 1841, is confirmatory of what we have above said on the subject of

Episcopacy in Sweden. *Fas est et ab hoste doceri.*

"In passing through London on my way to the United States of America, where at the earnest solicitation of the Rev. R. Baird, I hope to secure the sympathy and aid of various religious societies in behalf of Sweden, I heard the remark made, that the Swedish Church had not the proper apostolical succession, and could not therefore be acknowledged as a genuine Episcopal Church. Now, as it happens that a similar observation made some years ago by a distinguished prelate of this country, led to my carefully examining the historical facts of the case, I beg, in a few words, to place the result at your disposal, to make such use thereof as you may consider proper.

"Ansgarius (Anskar) who, in 830, first introduced the gospel into Sweden, was a regular clergyman of the then only Episcopal Church. When only thirty years of age he was, by the Emperor Louis, of France, appointed Archbishop of the Northern Churches, having his seat at Hamburg; and three years after the appointment was confirmed by the Pope, who named him legate for the same part of Europe. The whole management of the Northern Churches was under the direction of the Archiepiscopal see of Hamburg, until 1152, when the first Swedish Archbishop was appointed, having his residence at Lund. That the Reformation effected under the energetic and politic reign of the great Gustavus Vasa, did not in the slightest degree disturb the line of Episcopal ordination, will appear evident, not only from the fact that previously consecrated bishops continued in office notwithstanding the change, but more especially from the following remarkable circumstance. A vacancy occurring in the diocese of Westeras, just at the time when the Reformation was in progress, the Chapter nominated Petrus Magni, then residing as superior of a religious house at Rome. This being done, the King addressed a letter to the Pope, intimating the choice of the Chapter, and requesting as a favor that Petrus Magni might, at Rome itself, be consecrated to this Episcopal office, which was done accordingly. On his reaching Sweden, three other bishops elect were in readiness, and by the newly arrived bishop, assisted by others, consecrated to the holy office; one of these three was immediately made Archbishop of Upsala, and was no other than the famous Laurentius Petri, the father of the Reformation in Sweden.

"I may at some future time, be induced to give a more detailed account of the Swedish Church, the history of which is full of interest; but I could not refrain saying a few words now, in correction of an error, which probably has arisen by confounding the ecclesiastical affairs of Denmark with those of Sweden.

"In the former country the bishops were removed at the Reformation and superintendents introduced; in the latter, the Episcopal succession, as that form is ecclesiastically understood, is as clear and decided as in any part of the world. I, of course, view this subject only in its historical aspect, being perfectly convinced that the true apostolical succession must be made out in a very different way; but it is of some importance to rectify an error, and it may, with some in this country, place the Episcopal Church of Sweden in a more favorable light to be told the truth on this point.

"Believe me, dear sirs, yours truly,

GEO. SCOTT.

"London, April 19, 1841."

Palmer in his Church History (p. 150) says: "Episcopacy was never rejected by the Lutherans. They even retained the form of that Ecclesiastical government in several countries; and it is said that their Bishops in Sweden are validly ordained."

According to the Swedish canons, framed A. D. 1686, and which are still in force, *a priest cannot become a bishop without being conscecrated as such by bishops.*

Among the Symbola of the Swedish Church, is the *Decree of the Council of Upsala,* A. D. 1593, in which there is an acknowledgement and approval of the church ordinance, passed A.D. 1572. In this last it is expressly declared that the government of the church by bishops, is an order or arrangement "proceeding from God the Holy Ghost," and as such has been "universally approved and received in the whole of christendom, and as long as the world stands must continue."*

In view of the truth so apparent that the Swedish Church is Episcopal in its government, while it differs but little from the Protestant Episcopal Church in doctrine, it is not surprising that the Swedes on the Delaware, when their ecclesiastical connection with Sweden ceased, should with so much unanimity have come into union with the Episcopalians around them. They had, indeed, as all Episcopalians have, a fraternal regard for their brethren of the German Lutheran Church. In faith or doctrine there seems to be but little or nothing to keep us separate from each other. Had Luther been able to retain Episcopacy in Germany, in accomplishing that noble work which has given him so prominent a rank among the reformers of the church, we have no doubt that the Episcopalians and Lutherans of this country would long ere this have been one people.

Luther substituted parity for Episcopacy not from choice but from necessity. The Swedes, in introducing the Reformation, had the *Govern-*

*See letters of Rev. G. Unonius on the Church of Sweden, published a few years since in "The Gospel Messenger."

ment with them, and were therefore able to retain the Episcopal succession, or to exercise an influence having such a result. Luther, on the contrary, was *opposed* by the Government. Reformation in Germany had to make its way with the rulers generally, both civil and ecclesiastical, doing all in their power to suppress it. The Lutherans therefore of that country lost the Episcopal succession.

CHAPTER XII.

On the last Sunday of December, 1856, the rector of Gloria Dei church preached his twenty-fifth anniversary sermon. He took for his text Acts xiv. 27: "And when they were come, and had gathered the church together, they rehearsed all that God had done with them." A few extracts are here given from the sermon, for the purpose of showing the present condition of the parish, or the effect produced by the changes that have been made.

* * * "We come together to-day, as a church or congregation, to take a review of the twenty-five years now coming to a close, in which we have been associated as pastor and people. Twenty-five years! It is a quarter of a century! They number almost the years of a whole generation of men! * * When we revert to the time when I first entered this venerable church, to commence my labors among you, and remember who were then present, and look now at the congregation here assembled, how many are to-day absent who were then with us; *absent* as having been called, in the interim, into the world of spirits. In proof of this, we may merely refer to those who were the eight ves-

trymen of this church. Their names are familiar to some of you: John Douglas, Samuel Thackara, William Jones, William T. Smith, George L. Eyre, Matthias Coats, Charles Hidelius, and Henry Barry—*all gone,* except the venerable and valued friend last named.*

* * * "Death is always busy in calling away both old and young from this world to another. It has been my lot, in the twenty-five years I have been among you, to commit to the grave, in the solemn services of the church—some in our own yard, and some in others, besides funerals I have attended in company with other clergymen—eight hundred and three persons, of the various ages of human life.

* * * "The church in which we here worship is, as you all know, the oldest in Pennsylvania, by many years, having been erected A. D. 1700. During the one hundred and fifty-six years that the message of salvation has been proclaimed within its sacred courts, it has had twelve different rectors, averaging to each one a ministry of thirteen years.

* * * "When your rector took charge of this congregation, it was one of three congregations, all united under one charter; the other two being distant from this, the one six, and the other sixteen miles. This required his absence

*Since then, Mr. Barry has been also numbered with the dead.

from this church two Sundays in the month. * * * Assistant ministers, too, had to be employed, that each church might be open for service every Sunday.

"Under such a system, the prosperity and growth of the church were retarded and hindered. It was, therefore, as the result has shown, *wisely* determined, by the three congregations, to dissolve the connection, and to become three distinct and independent corporations. This was effected in the year 1843.

"The next step, taken two years later, was to bring this church into connection with the Protestant Episcopal Church in these United States. This, too, we think, was a wise measure, and though meeting at first with some little opposition, was soon acquiesced in by all the members of the parish.

"In looking back at the accomplishment of measures so important as these, and so certain to produce dissatisfaction in some minds, I feel rejoiced in being enabled to say that it occasioned little or no interruption in the harmony and the kindly feeling subsisting between myself and those who dissented from me in the policy or wisdom of those measures.

* * * "With regard to the union of this church with the Protestant Episcopal Church in this diocese and in the United States, it was a measure that did not require any sacrifice of principle, and that was demanded by con-

siderations involving the growth and prosperity of the parish. The Swedish Church, with which this church from its earliest origin had been in connection, is, and always has been, an *Episcopal* church. In making the change it was only substituting an Episcopal supervision *here at home*, and which could be given when required, for a *foreign* Episcopal supervision, which never had been and never could be adequately rendered.

"And as it was before an Episcopal church, so was it a church in the use of a *Liturgy*. Not a *different* liturgy from that we now use, but the same. The prayer book of the Episcopal Church—between which and the Swedish prayer book there is much resemblance—had for a long time been in use here under the former church government.

* * * "There has been a visible improvement in the growth and prosperty of the church since the change we are speaking of took place.

"Within the twenty-five years now closing there has been much done to improve the *property* of the church. Within that period the present parsonage has been erected,* a house purchased for the residence of the sexton, a two-story brick building put up for the accomodation of the Sunday schools, the organ now in

*The old parsonage, built in 1733, was torn down after the churches were separated and the property divided.

use purchased,* and the church itself, without any thing having been done to change at all its antique exterior, has, by important alterations and improvements, had its interior so changed, and modified and enlarged—and I may add *beautified*—by the erection of new pews and side galleries, the re-opening of the window in the rear of the pulpit, the enlarging of the chancel, and the placing therein of a new pulpit and lecturn, and in the mode of warming and lighting the church, as to adapt it to the improved condition and growing demands of the congregation.

"There has been expended in improvements, since the commencement of my ministry here, about twelve thousand dollars.

"We turn our attention now, for a few moments, to what God has done for us as regards the more direct results of ministeral labors.

"And first, with respect to the attendance that has been given upon the services of the church. * * * It has been a source of gratification to him who now addresses you that, though the attendance here at the commencement of his ministrations was but small, there has been a growth in the congregation that has brought the number of families connected with

* As this work is going to press, the vestry have ordered a new organ for the church.

the church up to one hundred and sixty, comprising some six hundred individuals.

* * * "The whole number of persons, children and adults, to whom, in the course of my ministry among you, I have administered the holy srcrament of baptism, has been one thousand nine hundred and thirty.

* * * "Although the Swedish Church recognizes the importance of confirmation, and at home is careful in seeing that her baptized members have their attention directed to it, in order to their renewing therein their baptismal engagements, I have seen no evidence to show that, before my own rectorship, it was ever administered in this church. The number of persons confirmed since 1834, when confirmation was first administered here, has been two hundred and seventy-five, averaging twelve to each year.

* * * "My first administration of the holy eucharist in this church was to about eight persons. The present number of communicants is one hundred and fifty.

* * * "The number of couples I have united in the bonds of matrimony, during my twenty-five years ministrations among you, has been one thousand three hundred and seventy-four.

"Let me speak, too, of our Sunday schools. These constitute an important element in a church's growth and prosperity. It is the children of the church who are to take their parents' places in the congregation when the latter are called away by death. And whether the parents are of the church or not, if we can train up their offspring in the way they should go, and implant the principles of religion in their tender minds, we shall be doing much to advance the future growth of the congregation. * * When I first came among you as your pastor, there was a male and female Sunday school here in successful operation. It has been my endeavor to sustain and carry forward these important nurseries of the church. In this work I have had, and still have, the aid and co-operation of many faithful teachers.* Our school at present numbers twenty-three teachers, and about two hundred and fifty scholars.

"Let me take this opportunity of expressing to you the gratification it has always afforded me in observing the attention shown by this congregation to strangers, in the visits they often pay to our church. It frequently happens that persons visiting for a while our city, feel desirous while here of attending some place or places of worship, that they may spend the Lord's day in the manner that God requires, and to which they have been accustomed at

*One of the male teachers now devoting himself in our school to the good work of training the young in the way they should go, was a teacher in the same school at the commencement here of my ministry. The labor of twenty-five years has not made him "weary in well doing."

home. What opinion must such persons form of the christian courtesy or politeness of a congregation in which they find themselves *ordered out* of the pew or pews into which they may enter. Or suppose a person caring but little about going to a place of worship, is induced in some way or other to enter one of our churches. He takes a seat, supposing, perhaps, as well he might, that the followers of Christ would be glad to see him coming to unite with them in the holy services of the sanctuary. But he finds himself mistaken. The renter of the pew comes to the door and gives him to understand that he is an intruder. He goes into another pew and is treated in the same manner. Indignant that persons having the name of christians should act thus, he leaves the church, and can never again be persuaded to enter it, or, perhaps, to enter *any other* place of worship. This is no mere fancy sketch, but exhibits what is known to have occurred in some congregations, and occurred with such results as I have mentioned. I rejoice to believe that in our own church visitors always receive a welcome to its services.

* * * "Our connection for twenty-five years as minister and people, has been marked by much that awakens in me feelings of gratification and thankfulness, in the harmony, and confidence and affection that have, with so little interruption, subsisted for so long a period

between us. We cannot look into the future and say how much longer this connection shall continue; but whatever may be its duration, let our prayer be that God may continue to prosper and to bless us, that the future in a greater degree than the past may be marked by his presence with us, and that the influences of his spirit may lead us onward to the final possession of that kingdom which he has prepared for those who love him. We may be sure that we shall have that presence if we are found faithful in the performance of the high and holy duties committed to us. The absence of prosperity from a church does not show want of faithfulness in God to his promises, but want of faithfulness in ourselves, in the right use of the means of grace vouchsafed to us. Let it be *my* endeavor to preach the truth as it is in Jesus, and *yours* to give it earnest attention and obedience, that when called to give an account of our stewardship, we may hear from the lips of the Judge the sentence, 'well done; enter ye into the joy of your Lord.'"

APPENDIX.

Note A.—Page 34.

"We, the underwritten, church wardens of the Wicaco congregation, salute our brethren, and notify that the Rev. Mr. Fabritius has now accomplished his official service promised for the year now ended; we therefore make a friendly request to each individual, by our agent, Jacob Yongh, that they may discharge their just debts to him without refusal. We also are solicitous to procure a further continuance of his services; and therefore desire that all who are willing for this, may subscribe respectively their voluntary contributions for his support, with their names or marks.

"Wicaco, 10th August, 1684."

One thousand and seventy-seven gilders were accordingly subscribed, making, in the currency of the country, as Mr. Rudman remarks, "at the rate of two gilders for a shilling, and four bushels of wheat at half a crown, the sum of £27 8*s.* 6*d.* This salary, with the aid of perquisites was at that time pretty good, but it was not well paid, and the old gentleman complained very much of the deficiency, especially in his latter time, as I have heard from persons of veracity."

Note B.—Page 35.

"The grace of God through Christ:

"Very reverend, very learned, very honorable Consistorial Senators of the unaltered Augsburgian Confession at Amsterdam:

"With a cordial and respectful salutation, we of the Swedish nation, in Pennsylvania, notify that the reverend and learned magister, Jacob Fabritius, who in 1677, on our vocation, commenced the clerical service, did, during five years, while having his eye-sight, and for nine years succeeding his loss of sight, diligently and faithfully attend us, by preaching and administering the sacraments, according to the orthodox Confession of Augsburg, and by an exemplary life; but must now resign his trust on account of blindness, and the infirmities of age. You will easily judge, venerable sirs, how forlorn will then be our situation! Like sheep without a shepherd—sick, without a physician —we shall be exposed to many dangers. We, therefore, supplicate you, in consideration of this, and our happy fellowship in the Lutheran Communion, to provide us with a proper Swedish character, as we know that many students of various nations are at Amsterdam, waiting for promotion (ordination.) And as a laborer is worthy of his reward, we stipulate for the coming minister a yearly salary of one hundred rix dollars, with a house and glebe for his maintenance. If a qualified person is not found at Amsterdam, we humbly request your kind aid to procure a clergyman from Sweden, by letters to the proper authorities."

Note C.—Page 44.

A list of the Swedish families residing in New Sweden in the year 1693, with the number of individuals in each family; taken from the document left by Mr. Rudman.

Heads of Families.	*Persons.*	*Heads of Families.*	*Persons.*
*Peter Rambo, Sen.	2	Lars Bure,	6
Peter Rambo, Jun.	6	Lars Johanson,	6
John Rambo,	6	Dirich Johanson,	5
Anders Rambo,	9	John Johnson,	2
Gunnar Rambo,	6	Peter Steelman,	4
Captain Lars Cock,	11	Frederick Konigh,	6
Eric Cock,	9	Elias Toy,	4
Mans Cock,	8	Johan Stelman,	4
Johan Cock,	7	Casper Fisck,	10
Gabriel Cock,	7	Staphan Ekhorn	5
*Anders Bengtson,	9	Peter Dalbo,	9
*Anders Bonde,	11	Otto Dalbo,	7
Sven Bonde,	5	Johan Matson,	11
*Johan Svenson,	9	*Antony Long,	5
Gunnar Svenson,	5	*Niels Matson,	3
*Michel Nielson,	11	*Israel Helm,	3
Anders Nielson,	3	*Anders Homman,	9
Brita Gostasson,	6	*Olle Dirickson,	7
Gosta Gostasson,	8	Anders Lock,	1
*Jonas Nielson,	4	Mans Lock,	1
Niels Jonason,	6	*Hans Petterson,	7
Mans Jonason,	3	*Hindrick Collman,	1
Anders Jonason,	4	*Johan Gostasson,	3
Jon Jonason,	2	Johan Hoppman,	7
Hans Joranson,	11	Frederick Hoppman,	7
*Mans Staake,	1	Anders Hoppman,	7
Peter Stake,	3	Nicholas Hoppman,	5
*Marten Martenson, Sen.	3	*Mans Hallton,	9
*Marten Martenson, Jun.	10	*Johan Anderson,	9
Mats Martenson,	4	Olle Pehrsson,	6
Otto Ernest Cock,	5	Lars Pehrsson,	1
Anders Persson Longaker,	7	*Hans Olofson,	5
Peter Jocom,	9	William Talley,	7
Johan Bonde,	1	Morten Knutssen,	6
Johan Schute,	4	Nils Trende's widow,	7
Mats Hollsten,	7	Anders Trende,	4
Johan Stille,	8	Reiner Peterson,	2
Anders Wihler,	4	Anders Hindrickson,	4
Mans Gostasson,	2	Johan Von Culen,	5
Niels Laican,	5	Hindrick Faske,	5
*Eric Mollica,	8	Johan Hindricsson,	5
Jonas Kyn, or Keen,	8	Johan Arien,	6
Mats Kyn,	3	William Cabb,	6
Bengt Bengtson,	2	Hans Keen's widow,	5
Christian Clason,	7	Chriestin Stalcop,	3
Niels Gastonberg,	3	Lucas Stedham,	7
Eric Gastonberg,	7	Lyloff Stedham,	9

Heads of Families.	Persons.	Heads of Families.	Persons.
Asmund Stedham,	5	Joran Joranson,	1
Adam Stedham,	8	Lorentz Osterson,	2
Benjamin Stedham,	7	*Johan Hindricson,	6
Brita Petterson,	8	David Hindricson,	7
Joran Anderson,	5	Carl Petterson,	5
*Broor Seneka,	7	Isaac Savoy,	7
Jesper Wallraven,	7	*Olle Fransson,	7
Jonas Wallraven,	1	Lars Petterson,	1
Conrad Constantine,	6	Mats Repott,	3
Olle Thomasson,	9	Olle Stoby,	3
Peter Palsson,	5	Mats Stark,	3
Johan Ommerson,	5	Johan Stalcop,	6
*Matthias De Foss,	6	Israel Stark,	1
Christiern Joransson,	1	*Paul Mink,	5
*Carl Springer,	5	Johan Schrage,	6
Johan Anderson,	7	Nils Repott,	3
*Hendrick Jacobson,	4	Hindrich Jacob,	1
James Van Der Weer,	7	Mats Jacob,	1
Cornelius Van Der Weer,	7	*Anders Sinnika,	5
William Van Der Weer,	1	Johan Hinderson, Jun.	3
Jacob Van Der Weer,	3	*Anders Weinom,	4
Hans Petterson,	5	Lars Larson,	1
Paul Petterson,	3	Hindric Danielson,	5
Peter Petterson,	3	Olle Thorson,	4
Peter Manson,	3	Jonas Skagge's widow,	6
Johan Manson,	5	Lars Tossa,	1
Hindrick Tossa,	5	Mats Tossa,	1
Johan Tossa,	4	*Staphan Jorason,	5
Thomas Johnson,	1	Lars Larson,	7
*Jaoob Clemson,	1	Joran Ericson,	1
*Olle Rosse,	5	Jacob Hindricson,	5
Jacob Closson,	6	Peter Lucason,	1
*Hindrick Anderson,	5	Lucas Lucason,	1
*Hindrick Iwarson,	9	Hans Lucason,	1
Johan Skrika,	1	*Olle Kuckow,	6
Mats Skirika,	3	Hindrich Slobey,	2
*Olle Paulsson,	9	Christopher Meyer,	7
Johan Steelman,	5	Hindrich Larsson,	7
Hindrick Parchon,	4	Mats Ericson,	3
*Simon Johanson,	10	Eric Ericson,	1
Johan Grantom,	3	Thomas Dennis,	6
Bengt Paulsson,	5	Anders Robertson,	3
Lasse Kempe,	6	Robert Longhorn,	4
Gostaf Paulsson,	6	*Anders Didricsson,	1
Hans Gostasson	7	Christiern Thomas' widow,	6
Peter Stalcop,	6	Paul Sahlunge,	3
Joran Bagman,	3	Lars Halling, or Huling,	1
Eric Joranson,	2		

Making 139 families.
939 individuals.

NOTE.—Of the foregoing list thirty-nine were native Swedes, of whom Peter Rambo and Andrew Bonde had been in this country fifty-four years. Those who were born in Sweden are distinguished by an asterisk, thus, *.

The reader will perceive how much the orthography of many of the above names has changed in the progress of time. Bengtsen is now Bankson; Bonde has become Boon; Svenson, Swanson; Cock, Cox; Gostasson, Justis; Jocum, Yocum; Hollsten, Holstein; Kyn, Keen; Hoppman, Hoffman; Von Culen, Culin; Halling, Hulings, or Hewlings; Wihler, Wheeler, etc. etc.

With regard to the Christian names, many of them correspond with our own, and merely show a difference in spelling and pronunciation between the two languages. Anders, therefore, among the Swedes, naturally became Andrew among us; Johan, John; Mats, Matthias, or Matthew: Carl, Charles; Bengt, Benjamin, or Benedict; Nils, Nicholas; Staphan, Stephen; Wilhelm, and also Olave, William; Hindrich, Henry; Michel, Michael; Jons, Jonathan, etc.

The river Delaware was called by the Swedes and Dutch, *South* river, in contradistinction to Hudson, or North river. Schuylkill, which signifies *hidden creek,* was so named from its mouth being concealed from view in passing up the Delaware. The Indians called it *Manaiung.* Many of the Swedish names of places are no longer retained, and it is difficult, in some instances, to identify them. *Amasland* is said by Acrelius to have been in Chester county, fifteen miles from Philadelphia. It was, probably, what is now called Upper Merion. *Kalkon-hook* still retains its Swedish name, and is below Darby.

Inquiry has been sometimes made as to the origin of the name, *Wicaco.* I suppose it to be of Indian origin. It may, however, have been given by the Swedes to this locality, as some of their names have a similar termination; as, *Wexio*, occurring in this volume, and presided over by one of their Bishops.

A Condensed View of the Ministers who successively presided over the Swedish Churches in America..

1. Reorus Torkillus accompanied Peter Menewe, who brought over the first Swedish colony, about the year 1636, and died here in 1643, aged thirty-five years.

2. John Campanius Holm came over in 1642 with Governor Printz, and remained here six years. Campanius was his proper surname—Holm having been added because of Stockholm having been his place of residence. He translated Luther's Catechism into the language of the Indians.

3. Laurence Lock came over in the time of Governor Printz. He preached at Tinicum and Christina. He was for many years the only clergyman the Swedes had. He died in 1688.

4. Israel Holg came about the year 1650, but did not remain long.

5. With Governor Rising, in 1652, a chaplain came over, and returned after the conquest of the Dutch in 1655.

6. Another clergyman came over in the ship Mercury, in the year 1656, and returned home two years afterwards.

7. Jacob Fabritius, who had been preaching for the Dutch in New York, was induced to settle among the Swedes, and preached his first

sermon at Wicaco in 1677. He officiated as their pastor for fourteen years, nine of which he was blind. He died about 1692.

Three clergymen arrived in 1697; from which period we may date the regular supply of the churches here with Swedish ministers. These were Andreas Rudman, Eric Biork, and Jonas Auren. The first settled at Wicaco, the second at Christina, and the third at Racoon and Penn's Neck.

WICACO CHURCH.

1. Andrew Rudman was the founder of the present church, which was built in 1700. In 1702 he went to preach for the Dutch in New York: afterwards officiated at Oxford church, near Frankford; then in Christ church, Philadelphia, where he died in 1708.

2. Andrew Sandel arrived in 1702. Returned home in 1719.

3. Jonas Lidman sent over in 1719. Recalled in 1730. The Rev. J. Eneberg took charge of the church during the vacancy.

4. Gabriel Falk appointed rector in 1733; deposed the same year.

5. John Dylander came over in 1737. He died honored and beloved, in 1741.

6. Gabriel Nesman appointed rector in 1743. Returned home in 1750.

7. Olof Parlin arrived in 1750; died in 1757.

8. Charles Magnus Wrangel came in 1759; returned in 1768; died 1786.

9. Andrew Goeranson, sent over in 1766; became rector 1768; officiated until the close of 1779; returned home in 1785: died in 1800.

10. Matthias Hultgren commenced his official duties in 1780; recalled in 1786.

11. Nicholas Collin, of Upsal, sent over in 1770; appointed to Wicaco 1786; died 1831. Close of the Swedish mission.

The present rector, Rev. J. C. Clay, D. D. was elected in December, 1831, and entered upon his duties the January following.

KINGSESSING CHURCH.

After the separation* of the three churches in 1843, the Rev. Samuel C. Brinckle was chosen rector of this church, and continued to officiate as such until 1850, when he was succeeded by the Rev. J. Brinton Smith. The latter resigned in 1856, and has been succeeded by the present rector, the Rev. Charles A. Maison.

UPPER MERION CHURCH.

The first rector of this church, after it became separated from the others, was the Rev. Ed-

* While the three churches were united as one corporation, the elections for vestrymen were held at Wicaco church. These elections, on account of the opposite views and interests of the different congregations often existing, frequently brought together a large number of voters, and produced great excitement. The separation of the churches has greatly tended to harmony and peace.

win N. Lightner. He resigned the parish in 1855, and the present rector, the Rev. William H. Rees, was chosen as his successor.

CHURCH AT CHRISTINA

1. Eric Biork built a new church at Fort Christina, in 1698, in lieu of that at Tranhook. Returned home 1714; died in 1740.

2. Andreas Hesselius, sent over in 1711; provost 1719; recalled in 1723; died in 1733.

3. Samuel Hesselius, brother to the former, sent over in 1729; returned 1731; died 1755.

4. John Eneberg, pastor, 1733; returned home in 1742.

5. Petrus Tranberg took charge of this church in 1742, and died in 1748.

6. Israel Acrelius, sent over in 1749; returned in 1756, died in 1800, aged eighty-six. He was the author of the work on the Swedish congregations in America.

7. Eric Unander, sent from Racoon and Penn's Neck to Christina in 1756.

8. Andreas Borell sent to preside over the Swedish churches in 1757; arrived here 1759; pastor in 1762; received the king's diploma, constituting him provost (præpositus) over all the Swedish churches here, where he died in 1768.

9. The Rev. Lawrence Girelius entered upon his duties as assistant October 1767; became provost of the churches in the place of the Rev.

Mr. Borell, in May, 1770. He continued in charge until 1791, when he returned to Sweden. He was the last of the Swedish ministers.

After the departure of the Rev. Mr. Girelius, the church at Christina became connected with the Protestant Episcopal church. For the following details with regard to the succession of Episcopal clergymen, who have officiated there, I am indebted to my friend, the Rev. Charles Breck, the present rector:

Rev.	Joseph Clarkson,	1792–1799.
"	William Pryce,	1800–1812.
"	Mr. Wickes,	1814–1817.
"	L. Bull, D. D.,	1818–1819.
"	Richard D. Hall,	1819–1822.
"	Ralph Williston,	1822–1826.
"	Pierce Connelly,	1827–1828.
"	Mr. Pardee,	1828–1835.
"	Mr. Adams,	1835–1838.
"	Dr. McCullough,	1838–1847.
"	Dr. Van Deusen,	1848–1852.
"	Charles Breck,	1853–

CHURCH AT RACOON AND PENN'S NECK.

The first minister was Polfladius. He was drowned in the Delaware in 1706.

1. Jonas Auren came over with Rudman and Biork, in 1697; appointed 1706; died in the exercise of his functions, 1713.

2. Abraham Lidenius, sent over in 1711; pastor 1714; returned home 1724; died 1728.

3. Petrus Tranberg and Andreas Windrufwa, sent over in 1726. They divided the churches between them, and so continued until 1728, when Windrufwa died. Between the time of Tranberg going to Christina, and his death in 1748, these churches had no pastor.

4. John Sandin appointed pastor 1748; died the same year.

5. Professor Kalm, travelling through North America under authority from the king of Sweden, supplied the church for a few months. He married the widow of Mr. Sandin, and returned to Sweden, after a perilous voyage.

6. Eric Unander, sent over in 1749; became pastor in 1751.

7. John Lidenius, (son of Abraham, abovementioned) appointed pastor in the place of Unander, 1756; died in Pennsylvania.

8. John Wicksell, sent over in 1760; arrived 1762; returned home 1774; died 1800.

9. Nicholas Collin, pastor 1778; appointed to Wicaco in 1786.—*See above.*

The following Clergymen have been at different times Assistant Ministers in the Swedish Churches.

The Rev. Charles Lute was appointed assistant to the Rev. Mr. Georgeson in 1774.

While Dr. Collin was rector, he had for his first assistant the Rev. Joseph Clarkson, who was appointed in 1787, and continued to officiate until 1792.

The Rev. Slator Clay was appointed in 1792, and officiated once a month in Upper Merion, and when there was a fifth Sunday in the month, at Kingsessing. Only part of his time was given to the Swedes, for whom he continued to preach until the day of his death, in 1821.

The Rev. Joseph Turner was appointed also in 1792, and was, for many years, connected with the Swedes, as one of their assistant ministers.

The Rev. J. C. Clay soon after his ordination in 1813, was called to the same churches, and officiated therein as an assistant for one year, when he was called to the churches at Norristown and Germantown.

The Rev. James Wiltbank was appointed to the same office in 1816, and performed its duties for four years, or until 1820.

The Rev. M. B. Roche in 1820 became an assistant minister to the Swedes, in which situation he officiated for a period of six months.

The Rev. J. C. Clay became a second time connected with these churches in 1822, having been appointed an assistant for Upper Merion church, in connection with the Norristown and Perkiomen churches.* He also officiated on every fifth Sunday, or four times a year, at Kingsessing. He continued to fill this station until called in 1831 to the rectorship.

The Rev. Charles M. Dupuy was, in 1822, appointed the assistant for Wicaco and Kingsessing, and was continued as such until 1828.

The Rev. Pierce Connelly† succeeded Mr. Du-

* From 1817 to 1822 he had charge for the first of these years of the Church and Academy in Newbern, North Carolina, and the remainder of the time, (4 years) of the Church at Hagerstown, Maryland, when, upon the death of his father, the Rev. Slator Clay, he was called to the church at Perkiomen, and also a second time to that at Norristown.

† The election of Mr. Connelly as assistant minister at Wicaco, was in opposition to the wishes of many of the congregation. This opposition was carried so far as to determine some of them to prevent his officiating in the church. When, therefore, he was to hold his first service, a few leading individuals interrupted him as often as he attempted to commence the service, and created such a disturbance as to induce him to invite the congregation into the Grave Yard, in order to his officiating from one of the tomb-stones. But he encountered the same opposition there, and was obliged to give up the thought of holding service on that occasion. A suit was brought in one of our courts, by the vestry, against those who had created this disturbance of the worship of the church, and a verdict obtained against them, but at the request of the vestry, there was but a light penalty imposed.

puy, and officiated chiefly at Kingsessing, though part of the time at Wicaco also, till the close of 1831, when he accepted a call to Natchez, Mississippi.

The Rev. Raymond A. Henderson was chosen assistant to the Rev. J. C. Clay in 1832, and continued in the churches until the close of 1834, when he was called to the French Protestant Church in New Orleans.

The Rev. John Reynolds was assistant for one year at Upper Merion, having been appointed about the same time with Mr. Henderson.

After the two last mentioned, the Rev. William Diehl and the Rev. Samuel C. Brinckle acted as assistants until the churches were separated.

FINIS.

www.ingramcontent.com/pod-product-compliance
Lightning Source LLC
LaVergne TN
LVHW010742120826
845150LV00009B/1572

* 9 7 8 1 4 2 5 5 1 5 1 2 6 *